# GOD IN THE WHITE HOUSE: A HISTORY

# GOD IN THE WHITE HOUSE: A HISTORY

How Faith Shaped the Presidency
from John F. Kennedy to George W. Bush

## Randall Balmer

HarperOne
*An Imprint of HarperCollinsPublishers*

HarperOne

GOD IN THE WHITE HOUSE: *A History: How Faith Shaped the Presidency from John F. Kennedy to George W. Bush.* Copyright © 2008 by Randall Balmer. All rights reserved. Printed in the United States of America. No part of this book may be used or reproduced in any manner whatsoever without written permission except in the case of brief quotations embodied in critical articles and reviews. For information address HarperCollins Publishers, 10 East 53rd Street, New York, NY 10022.

HarperCollins books may be purchased for educational, business, or sales promotional use. For information please write: Special Markets Department, HarperCollins Publishers, 10 East 53rd Street, New York, NY 10022.

HarperCollins Web site: http://www.harpercollins.com

HarperCollins®, 📖®, and HarperOne™ are trademarks of HarperCollins Publishers

FIRST HARPERCOLLINS PAPERBACK EDITION PUBLISHED IN 2008

Library of Congress Cataloging-in-Publication Data is available upon request.

ISBN 978–0–06–087258–8

09 10 11 12 13 RRD(H) 10 9 8 7 6 5 4 3 2 1

*For Andrew*
*from his very proud father*

Fame is a vapor, popularity an accident,
Riches take wing, and only character endures.

—HORACE GREELEY

Congress shall make no law respecting an establishment of religion, or prohibiting the free exercise thereof . . .

. . . no religious test shall ever be required as a qualification to any office or public trust under the United States.

UNITED STATES CONSTITUTION

# CONTENTS

# PREFACE

This book aspires to answer a relatively simple question: How did we get from John F. Kennedy's eloquent speech at the Rice Hotel in Houston on September 12, 1960, in which he urged voters effectively to bracket a candidate's faith out of their considerations when they entered the voting booth, to George W. Bush's declaration on the eve of the 2000 Iowa precinct caucuses that Jesus was his favorite philosopher?

A simple question, perhaps, but the answer is rather more complex. Any responsible attempt to solve this puzzle must take into account the shifting tectonics of ethnic and religious prejudices, the extent to which religious convictions did (or did not) affect policy, various presidential scandals, the appeal of candidates viewed as outsiders to Washington, the politicization of evangelical voters, and the probity of individual presidents. Presidential politics over the course of these four-plus decades, 1960 to 2004, saw the election of the first Roman Catholic to the presidency, the first presidential resignation, the first man to ascend to the Oval Office who had never been elected either president or vice president, the first president who claimed to be a "born again" Christian, the first woman and (later) the first Jew on a major-party ticket, the first all-Southern Baptist presidential and vice-presidential ticket, and only the second presidential impeachment in American history.

These forty-four years also saw some of the closest presidential elections in American history—Kennedy-Nixon in 1960, Nixon-Humphrey in 1968, Bush-Gore in 2000, and Bush-Kerry in 2004—as well as some of the most lopsided results—Johnson-Goldwater in 1964, Nixon-McGovern in 1972, and Reagan-Mondale in 1984. Two successful candidates over the course of these four decades, Jimmy Carter and George W. Bush, offered themselves to the voters as "redeemer presidents," promising to cleanse the temple of the White House of the sins of their predecessors.

In other words, it was an eventful four-plus decades in presidential politics, and attitudes about religion, specifically about the candidates' faith, have varied widely over that span of time, from studied indifference to careful scrutiny. Briefly, the narrative arc of these forty-four years looks something like this:

Kennedy, acting out of political necessity and seeking to displace the Protestant establishment in 1960, argued that a candidate's religion was not a legitimate criterion for voting decisions, an argument that endured for more than a decade, until the Watergate scandal forced Richard Nixon's resignation in 1974. Jimmy Carter, a Washington outsider who offered himself as a redeemer president, reintroduced matters of faith and belief into the arena of public discourse. For a variety of reasons, not least the rise of the Religious Right in the late 1970s, many of the same evangelical voters who had helped propel Carter into office turned emphatically against him four years later in favor of Ronald Reagan, who also claimed to be an evangelical Christian. Since 1980, with the single exception of the Clinton presidency, candidates who have made forthright professions of evangelical faith and who have enjoyed the support of Religious Right leaders have occupied the Oval Office. Even the Clinton "aberration" might be explained by Bill Clinton's extraordinary skills as a politician and by his ability to speak the evangelical language of sin and redemption—this despite the fact that leaders of the Religious Right utterly despised him and did everything in their power to discredit him. George W. Bush's narrow victory in 2000 can be viewed as an attempt by voters to cleanse the Oval Office of Clinton's personal transgressions, just as Carter's election in 1976 represented an attempt to purge the nation of Nixon-era corruptions.

All of this is not to suggest that faith or religion played a singular, much less a decisive, role in any of these elections. Not at all. Every campaign—every presidency—rises and falls on the waves of political circumstances and historical vicissitudes as well as such nebulous factors as personal charisma, economic conditions, and the shifting sands of public opinion. Still, the fact remains that Americans were content to disregard religion as a criterion for voting in 1960, whereas by 2004 they had come to expect candidates fully to disclose their religious views and to expound on their personal relationship to the Almighty.

This book attempts to trace that transition.

I should also say a word about what this book is not. It does not pretend to be a comprehensive history of how religion has shaped the presidency or presidential campaigns from 1960 to 2004. I do not scrutinize, for example, how every attitude toward, say, civil rights or women's rights or every policy decision affecting

*[handwritten marginal note: "idea of 'redeemer Presidents'"]*

the Middle East might or might not be dictated by a president's religious convictions. Nor do I devote much attention to polling data to determine popular attitudes. It's not that I distrust polls or pollsters—well, maybe I do. As Mark Twain once observed, the world is rife with "lies, damned lies, and statistics." So much depends on how questions are formulated, and I think it's especially dicey to determine people's religious attitudes because nomenclature tends to be fraught—who is or is not a Christian, for instance, or an evangelical. I'll leave the numbers to the statisticians and to the political scientists.

Nor do I talk much about "civil religion," the conflation of religious devotion with nationalistic symbols. It's not that I dispute the existence of civil religion. It's just that discussion of the matter long ago passed from exhaustive to tiresome, and I don't think, frankly, that it adds all that much to this account.

I offer instead a narrative that tells the story not only of the politicization of religion in the final decades of the twentieth century, but also the "religionization" of our politics. I reflect, finally, on the implications of this shift, which has reverberated in both worlds, religious and political.

Although I recognize that no author can be entirely objective, I have tried very hard to be fair. For those anxious to sort out my sympathies, I'll make it easy. I consider myself an evangelical Christian whose understanding of the teachings of Jesus points him toward the left of the political spectrum. I am no fan of the Religious Right, whose leaders, I believe, have distorted the gospel—the "good news"—of the New Testament and have defaulted on the noble legacy of nineteenth-century evangelical activism, which invariably took the part of those less fortunate.

I am not arguing, however, that people of faith should not be involved in the political process. Far from it. I happen to believe that the arena of public discourse would be impoverished without voices of faith. And, although I don't think it's necessary, I have no particular problem with political candidates offering their religious views to public scrutiny. At the same time, however, I think there is a real danger to the integrity of the faith when it is aligned too closely with a particular political movement or political party, because the faith then loses its prophetic voice. My reading of American religious history suggests that religion always functions best from the margins of society, not in the councils of power.

That, I believe, is only one of the cautionary lessons from the final four decades of the twentieth century.

JfK's speech to GHMA

John F. Kennedy taking questions from members of the Greater Houston Ministerial Association on September 12, 1960. Kennedy's speech implored Americans to bracket a candidate's faith out of their considerations when they entered the voting booth. The "Kennedy paradigm" of indifference toward a candidate's religion persisted until the 1976 presidential election.

ONE

# PROTESTANT UNDERWORLD

*John F. Kennedy and the "Religious Issue"*

On a Monday evening, September 12, 1960, the junior senator from the commonwealth of Massachusetts approached the dais in the ballroom of the Rice Hotel in downtown Houston. "While the so-called religious issue is necessarily and properly the chief topic here tonight," John F. Kennedy began, "I want to emphasize from the outset that we have far more critical issues to face in the 1960 election." The Democratic nominee for president had just completed another hot, exhausting day of campaigning across the state of Texas. Together with his running mate, Senator Lyndon B. Johnson, Kennedy had already visited El Paso, Lubbock, and San Antonio in what the *New York Times* characterized as "the largest aerial campaign armada in history."[1]

Kennedy had been greeted by "tumultuous cheers from many thousands of Texans" that day, but his reception at the Rice Hotel was

---

1. "Kennedy Team Cheered," *New York Times,* September 13, 1960.

noticeably more tepid. "I believe in an America that is officially neither Catholic, Protestant nor Jewish," Kennedy continued, "where
no public official either requests or accepts instructions on public
policy from the pope, the National Council of Churches or any other
ecclesiastical source—where no religious body seeks to impose its
will directly or indirectly upon the general populace or the public
acts of its officials—and where religious liberty is so indivisible that
an act against one church is treated as an act against all."[2]

Kennedy issued a ringing endorsement of the separation of
church and state that evening—"I believe in an America where
the separation of church and state is absolute," he said—but he
clearly wanted to be addressing issues other than religion. And
by standing before the gathered members of the Greater Houston
Ministerial Association, the Democratic nominee had entered the
belly of the beast. Houston was not exactly friendly territory for
a Roman Catholic running for president, and the events of the
preceding weeks clearly had frustrated the young senator, who
had hoped that, by this late stage in the campaign, he would have
been able to shrug off what was almost universally described as
the "religious issue."

Kennedy, of course, was not the first Roman Catholic
in American history to run for the presidency. In 1928 Alfred
E. Smith, the governor of New York, had won the Democratic
nomination and the right to square off against Herbert Hoover,
secretary of commerce under Calvin Coolidge and the Republican nominee. In December 1923, as Smith was gearing up for an
earlier run at the Democratic nomination, William MacDonald,

---

2. "Kennedy Team Cheered." For the full text of Kennedy's speech, see Appendix 1.

pastor of the First Presbyterian Church in Queens, New York, had organized an anti-Smith rally. Five thousand people attended, according to the *New York Times;* MacDonald led the congregation in the singing of "Stand Up for Jesus" as white-robed Klansmen processed into the auditorium. A particular Klansman, known as the "Human Dynamo," concluded his remarks by shouting, "Thank God there are six million people in the United States who have pledged their lives that no son of the Pope of Rome will ever sit in the Presidential chair!" Several days later, two fire companies were summoned to tear down a flaming cross, twenty-five feet high and fifteen feet wide at the crossbar, near the site of the Klan rally.[3]

In the course of the 1928 campaign, Smith sought to defuse the issue of his religious affiliation with a speech in Oklahoma City, but his Catholicism continued to dog him throughout the campaign. He tangled with John Roach Straton, the arch-fundamentalist pastor of Calvary Baptist Church in New York City, who identified the Democratic candidate with "the forces of vice, lawlessness and drunkenness." Nativist groups charged that Smith would be a tool of the Vatican, and scurrilous pamphlets warned that as president, Smith would annul Protestant marriages and establish Roman Catholicism as the religion of the United States. Although the Democratic platform promised "an honest effort to enforce" Prohibition, Smith's long-standing opposition to the Eighteenth Amendment revived the nineteenth-century nativist associations between "Rum and Romanism." Hoover, on the other hand, defended Prohibition as "a great

---

3. "Cross Is Fired Near Scene of Klan Attack on Smith," *New York Times,* December 21, 1923.

social and economic experiment noble in motive and far-reaching in purpose." In the traditionally Democratic South, the Ku Klux Klan campaigned for Hoover, a Quaker, and against the Roman Catholic.[4]

When Hoover won decisively in the 1928 election—58 percent of the popular vote and 444 to 77 in the electoral college—popular lore had it that Smith sent a one-word telegram to the Vatican: "UNPACK."

Protestant suspicions of Roman Catholicism, however, refused to abate. The fact that the sons of Catholic immigrants enlisted for military service during World War II demonstrated their patriotism, even though they sometimes fought against the countries from which their parents and grandparents emigrated. The G.I. Bill of Rights, passed by Congress in 1944, provided these same second-generation immigrants the opportunity to attend college and thereby to toe the first rung on the ladder of upward mobility toward the middle class.

Many American Catholics made that ascent in the postwar years, but not without resistance. In 1949 nativism once again reared its ugly head. In March of that year, Beacon Press, a liberal publisher in Boston, issued the first edition of Paul Blanshard's *American Freedom and Catholic Power.* "When a church enters the arena of controversial social policy and attempts to control the judgment of its own people (and of other people) on foreign af-

---

4. Quoted in "Smith Demands Straton Let Him Answer Attack in Church; Pastor Willing," *New York Times,* August 8, 1928; David Burner, *Herbert Hoover, A Public Life* (New York: Knopf, 1979), 218. Straton also indicated in his sermon that, although he generally voted Democratic, he would not vote for Smith, the Democratic nominee for president.

*[handwritten annotation: Paul Blanshard believed Catholics would fuse american foreign policy w/ Vatican interests.]*

fairs, social hygiene, public education and modern science," the author warned, "it must be reckoned with as an organ of political and cultural power." The book cited Catholic efforts to oppose birth control and divorce laws, noted the segregation of Catholic children into parochial schools, and suggested that the political muscle of American Catholics was being exerted "to bring American foreign policy into line with Vatican temporal interests."[5]

What made Blanshard's treatise so remarkable was its provenance. Unlike the sensationalist nineteenth-century nativist literature, much of which salaciously conjured the supposed goings-on in Catholic convents, Blanshard was both a journalist and an attorney, educated at Michigan, Harvard, and Columbia. He viewed himself not as a reactionary nativist, but as a liberal who was concerned that "a misunderstanding of the nature of tolerance" represented a real "danger to the democratic way of life." *American Freedom and Catholic Power* pointed out that "the Catholic people are not citizens but subjects in their own religious commonwealth," which rendered Catholicism inimical to democracy. "The secular as well as the religious policies of their Church are made in Rome by an organization that is alien in spirit and control," Blanshard warned, and Catholics "are compelled by the very nature of their Church's authoritarian structure to accept nonreligious as well as religious policies that have been imposed on them from abroad."[6]

*[handwritten annotation: So DUMB]*

---

5. Paul Blanshard, *American Freedom and Catholic Power* (Boston: Beacon Press, 1949), 3, 4. Mark Massa examines the importance of Blanshard's book at various points in *Catholics and American Culture: Fulton Sheen, Dorothy Day, and the Notre Dame Football Team* (New York: Crossroad, 1999).

6. Blanshard, *American Freedom*, 4, 5.

*American Freedom and Catholic Power* became a best-selling book; Beacon Press ordered eleven printings in as many months. So when a Roman Catholic senator from Massachusetts began mulling a run for the presidency in the 1950s, the experience of Alfred Smith and the lingering anti-Catholicism evident in the popularity of Blanshard's book was very much on his mind. Paradoxically, Kennedy himself was not particularly devout, unlike his mother. His reputation for womanizing, both before and after his marriage in 1953, may not have been widely known, but it was locally known. "I think it's so unfair of people to be against Jack because he's Catholic," Jacqueline Kennedy said of her husband during the 1960 campaign. "He's such a poor Catholic."[7]

Kennedy, having supported the nomination of Adlai Stevenson, flirted with the notion of being the vice-presidential nominee in 1956. Indeed, the idea had won some support from newspaper editorial pages, in part because Kennedy's strong identity as a Roman Catholic, it was argued, might blunt some of the criticism directed at Stevenson for having been divorced. But other Democratic leaders believed that Kennedy's religion would doom a Stevenson-Kennedy ticket.

According to Theodore Sorensen, the senator's longtime aide and speechwriter, Kennedy was initially ambivalent about the vice-presidential slot, but, in view of a possible bid for the White House in the future, Kennedy did not want to be excluded from consideration solely because of his faith. Sorensen produced

7. Quoted in Garry Wills, *Bare Ruined Choirs: Doubt, Prophecy, and Radical Religion* (New York: Doubleday, 1972), 80–81.

a document, which was artfully leaked to the media, show-ing that a Catholic on the national ticket actually could enhance Stevenson's prospects. Sorensen later insisted that it was by no means an objective study; rather, it was "a political answer to the sweeping assertions made against nominating a Catholic for Vice President." Regardless of the outcome at the 1956 Democratic National Convention—Senator Estes Kefauver of Tennessee got the vice-presidential nod—the "Bailey Memorandum," as it was known (for political reasons, the Kennedy camp attributed it to John Bailey, chair of the state Democratic committee in Connecti-cut), "at least reopened the previously closed assumption that a Catholic on the ticket spelled defeat."[8]

As Kennedy considered his own run for the presidency, he was well aware that religion would factor into the equation and that he would have to pursue the nomination determinedly. "If I were governor of a large state, Protestant and fifty-five," he re-marked, "I could sit back and let it come to me." Kennedy sought repeatedly to bracket the issue of his faith from his candidacy, offering assurances of his opposition to the use of taxpayer money for religious schools and emphasizing the presidential oath to uphold the Constitution. He cited both the First Amendment, which enshrined the notion of church-state separation, as well as Article VI of the Constitution, which prohibited any religious test for officeholders. In a letter to Harold Brown, president of the Oregon Council of Churches, Kennedy elaborated on his under-standing of the disestablishment clause of the First Amendment: "Under the First Amendment our government cannot—directly

---

8. Theodore C. Sorensen, *Kennedy* (New York: Harper & Row, 1965), 83.

or indirectly, carelessly or intentionally—select any religious body for either favorable or unfavorable treatment."[9]

As the prospect of a presidential candidacy by a Roman Catholic in 1960 began to look more and more likely, a group of Jewish and Christian leaders organized themselves into an entity called the Fair Campaign Practices Committee. The organization included prominent rabbis, Catholics, various Orthodox and Protestant leaders, and Carl F. H. Henry, editor of *Christianity Today,* the flagship magazine of evangelicalism. The group also included George Romney, a Mormon and the president of American Motors, who would be elected governor of Michigan in 1962 and who would mount his own candidacy for the Republican presidential nomination in 1968. The Fair Campaign Practices Committee met at the Mayflower Hotel in Washington on March 24–25, 1960, to prepare a "Special Statement on Religion in the 1960 Campaign."

The statement articulated five "simple principles which we hope will commend themselves to American voters." The Kennedy camp could hardly have hoped for more. "It is proper and desireable [*sic*] that every public official should attempt to govern his conduct by a personal conscience informed by his religious faith," the statement began. "No candidate for public office should be opposed or supported because of his particular religious affiliation," it continued. "A campaign for a public office is not an opportunity to vote for one religion against an-

---

9. Quoted in Sorenson, *Kennedy,* 97, 109; Letter, G. Bromley Oxnam to John F. Kennedy, April 20, 1959, "Church and State" folder, Pre-Presidential Papers, Senate Files, Box 535, John F. Kennedy Library; "The Religious 'Issue' in the Presidential Campaign," circular "Authorized and paid for by the District of Columbia Committee for John F. Kennedy," John F. Kennedy Library.

other." The statement concluded with admonitions against "stirring up, fostering, or tolerating religious animosity" and calling instead for "intelligent, honest, and temperate public discussion of the relation of religious faith to the public issues."[10]

Kennedy worked hard to neutralize the religious issue in advance of the campaign. "Whatever one's religion in his private life may be," Kennedy told *Look* magazine in 1959, "for the officeholder nothing takes precedence over his oath to uphold the Constitution and all its parts—including the First Amendment and the strict separation of church and state." Kennedy added, "The First Amendment to the Constitution is an infinitely wise one."[11]

As early as April 1959, the senator from Massachusetts met with a delegation of Methodist bishops. Afterward, one of the bishops assured Kennedy that "the church a man belongs to ought not to be the decisive factor in a political situation." Rather, he continued, "It is his belief, his record, his character, his word that really counts." Even Paul Blanshard, author of *American Freedom and Catholic Power,* weighed in on the Democratic senator from Massachusetts. "Regardless of one's attitude toward Kennedy the candidate," Blanshard wrote in 1959, ten years after the release of his book, "Kennedy the Catholic deserves credit for speaking out

10. Bulletin of the Fair Campaign Practices Committee, Inc. [mimeograph], April 1, 1960, "Religious Issue: Correspondence" folder, Robert F. Kennedy Papers, Pre-Administration Political Files, General Subject Files, 1959–60, Box 47, John F. Kennedy Library.

11. Quoted in James Reston, "The Catholicism Issue," *New York Times,* December 16, 1959.

with candor on the side of the Supreme Court's interpretation of the Constitution concerning the payment of public funds for the central activities of sectarian schools."[12]

When Kennedy stepped to the podium on January 2, 1960, however, to announce his candidacy for the Democratic nomination, he recognized that the religion issue would bedevil him unless he found a way somehow to neutralize it. He tried a number of strategies to do so, including humor. At the 1959 annual Alfred E. Smith dinner in New York, a rite of passage for presidential aspirants, Kennedy had reminded the audience of a previous election that he thought had special relevance to the 1960 presidential campaign looming on the horizon. "I think it well that we recall what happened to a great governor when he became a Presidential nominee," he began. "Despite his successful record as governor, despite his plain-spoken voice, the campaign was a debacle. His views were distorted. He carried fewer states than any candidate in his party's history. To top it off, he lost his own state that he had served so well as a governor." Kennedy paused. "You all know his name and his religion," he said solemnly. "Alfred F. Landon, Protestant."[13]

Many Protestants in the run-up to the 1960 campaign refused to budge from their conviction that a Roman Catholic should never occupy the Oval Office. "Senator Kennedy's active

---

12. Letter, Paul Blanshard to *Washingon Post,* March 27, 1959.

13. Quoted in Paul F. Boller Jr., *Presidential Campaigns: From George Washington to George W. Bush* (New York: Oxford University Press, 2004), 296. Toward the end of the presidential campaign in 1960, after Harry Truman, in his characteristically salty language, told Southerners that if they voted for Nixon they could go to hell, Kennedy allowed, tongue-in-cheek, that Democrats should "try to refrain from raising the religious issue" (Boller, *Presidential Campaign,* 300).

participation in the presidential nomination, in our opinion, is almost certain to result in his failure to receive the coveted post at the Democratic national convention," an editorial in the *Olewein* (Iowa) *Register* noted just days after his announcement. The editorial articulated an anxiety apparently shared by many Americans, namely that a Roman Catholic president "would place the instructions of his church above public duty." A Lutheran pastor from Eau Claire, Wisconsin, expressed similar concerns. "I would find great difficulty in my Conscience if I were to vote for a member of the Roman denomination," he wrote in his parish paper. "And the history of the Roman church and its 'meddling' in government at all levels is not a pretty picture."[14]

The initial showdown over religion occurred in West Virginia. Back in December 1959, Kennedy's pollster, Louis Harris, assured him that he enjoyed a 70 to 30 percent edge over Hubert Humphrey, his principal rival for the nomination, in the state. Although there was no compelling reason for Kennedy to enter the West Virginia primary—the election was not binding on the delegates—the Kennedy camp saw it as an opportunity to force a confrontation with Humphrey; if Kennedy could prevail in an overwhelmingly Protestant state, then the campaign could put to rest the notion that a Roman Catholic could not be elected president.

That strategy very nearly backfired. Three weeks before the May 10 primary, the growing public awareness of Kennedy's religion prompted almost a complete reversal of the earlier poll

---

14. Editorial, *Oelwein* (Iowa) *Register,* January 8, 1960; "From the Pastor's Study," Grace Lutheran Parish Paper (Eau Claire, Wisconsin), March 10, 1960, "Catholic Issue" folder, Pre-Presidential Papers, 1960 Campaign, Box 1044, John F. Kennedy Library.

numbers: 60 to 40 percent in favor of Humphrey. The Kennedy machine went into full operation, but the issue of the candidate's faith hung like the sword of Damocles over the entire campaign.

Some of Kennedy's advisers urged him to address the matter directly, while others counseled him not to call attention to it. "A number of your friends in the Cambridge community have asked me to urge you once more to consider making a very serious, full-dress speech upon the relationship between Church and State," Archibald Cox of Harvard wrote to Kennedy. "Although nothing can be said which will impress the prejudiced, there is a sizable group of thoughtful people who are seriously troubled about the prospect of having a President whose religion is what they regard as authoritarian. Their doubts are far more serious than such silly questions as the weight of the Vatican upon our domestic or foreign policies for they deal with such philosophical questions as intellectual freedom." Cox urged Kennedy to deliver a speech that would "stress the development of our American tradition of the separation of Church and State in the light of the institutions of other countries," even as it made "the affirmative case for religion as part of a nation's life and culture."[15]

The candidate chose to confront the issue. "I need your help in my campaign for President of the United States in the West Virginia Primary," a letter to West Virginia Democrats read. "But there are some who would not give me a chance to put that program into effect simply because I go to the church of my parents on Sunday." Then, on Sunday evening, May 8, two days before

---

15. Letter, Archibald Cox to John F. Kennedy, April 8, 1960, "Religious Issue: Campaign Material" folder 2, Theodore C. Sorenson Papers, Campaign Files, 1959–60, Box 25, John F. Kennedy Library.

the primary, Kennedy made what presidential historian Theodore White called "the finest TV broadcast I have ever heard any political candidate make." Kennedy affirmed the notion of the separation of church and state and then, looking directly into the camera, talked about the oath a president makes to uphold the Constitution, including the First Amendment. "And if he breaks his oath," Kennedy solemnly declared, "he is not only committing a crime against the Constitution, for which the Congress can impeach him—and should impeach him—but he is committing a sin against God."[16]

Kennedy won West Virginia the following Tuesday and the Nebraska primary the same day. Humphrey promptly pulled out of the race for the Democratic nomination. "I think," Kennedy declared at his victory press conference in Charleston, West Virginia, "we have now buried the religious issue once and for all."[17]

A coterie of determined Protestants had other ideas. Kennedy's candidacy resurrected all manner of scurrilous anti-Catholic rhetoric, which frequently took form in various tracts, many of them printed and distributed anonymously. "Don't let any Catholic convince you that his oath to his State or Government comes first," a mimeographed broadside read. "A Catholic is bound to his Church from infancy. Therefore his Church comes first in all

---

16. Letter draft, John F. Kennedy to West Virginia Democrats, April 18, 1960, "Religion" folder, Pre-Presidential Papers, 1960 Campaign, Box 997, John F. Kennedy Library; Theodore H. White, *The Making of the President 1960* (New York: Athenaeum, 1962), 107–8.

17. Quoted in White, *Making of the President 1960*, 114.

things." This pamphlet, purportedly written and distributed by J. F. Murphy of Boston, who described himself as a "Sincere Free-Thinking Catholic," warned that a Roman Catholic elected to the presidency would appoint only Catholics to his cabinet. "After that every key Government head would also be a Catholic," the attack read. "Within one four-year term as President, America would be under full Catholic control. The Pope wants rich America under Catholic control. All other Catholic-controlled countries are poor, and always have been."[18]

"A CATHOLIC PRESIDENT? No, I'm sorry. It would be like voting for a Fascist, a Nazi, in one respect." So read another broadside, this one from Menomonee Falls, Wisconsin. A tract published by an organization calling itself the Conversion Center, in Havertown, Pennsylvania, also resurrected the specter of fascism, an accusation that still carried considerable potency among a people with lingering memories of the Second World War: "The Roman Catholic Hierarchy is conducting a massive campaign to hide its true doctrines, and to gain public sympathy. It is using the doctrine of the 'Big Lie,' employed so successfully by Hitler and Stalin."[19]

As Kennedy closed in on the Democratic nomination, a flurry of tracts appeared. This one, purportedly written by a

---

18. Mimeographed letter, J. F. Murphy, Boston ["Sincere Free-Thinking Catholic"] to "All Who Love America and Religious Freedom," n.d., "Catholic Issue" folder, Pre-Presidential Papers, 1960 Campaign, Box 1044, John F. Kennedy Library.

19. Ditto letter, Kenneth F. Klinkert, Menomonee Falls, Wisconsin, n.d., "Catholic Issue" folder, Pre-Presidential Papers, 1960 Campaign, Box 1044, John F. Kennedy Library; Tract, "Who Says Refusal to Vote for a Roman Catholic Presidential Candidate Is Bigotry?" published by The Conversion Center, Inc., Havertown, Pennsylvania, "Catholic Issue" folder, Pre-Presidential Papers, 1960 Campaign, Box 1044, John F. Kennedy Library.

"Converted Roman Catholic Priest," spelled out the dimensions of the supposed Vatican conspiracy:

## DID YOU KNOW

That the Roman papal hierarchy is an enemy to our American government, and an enemy in disguise, in that it is a corrupt foreign political machine operating under the mask of religion?

That the Roman papal hierarchy seeks to destroy our free public schools, to do away with free speech, free press, soul liberty and to force its oriental, ancient, superstitious, idolatrous, un-Christian practices upon the nation?

That the forceable [sic] enslavement and incarceration of women in Roman nunneries is a blot on the good name of America and is certainly a shame to twentieth century civilization?

That a Roman Catholic president in the White House is the next step planned by the hierarchy of enthroned cardinals, bishops and priests?

That Rome looks upon Washington as the future center of her power, and is filling our government departments with papists?

... And this group take their orders from the man-god in the Vatican at Rome trying to make America Roman Catholic, capture the White House and rule over the

United States of this great Protestant nation. In Christ's name, Americans awaken—stand guard—it shall not be so—"They Shall Not Pass."

The tract concluded with an almost desperate admonition: "Scatter this tract quickly. Put one in every letter you write. Help us defeat the Roman political machine from 'Making America Catholic.'"[20]

"Doubtlessly all our readers are aware that this is an election year, and one of the avowed candidates for the Democratic nomination is a Romanist," the editor of the *Baptist Examiner,* published out of Russell, Kentucky, began. "I hardly think that our country is ready to elect a Roman Catholic president as yet, but we need to be warned, and the alarm needs to go out concerning Roman Catholicism." The editor protested that he had "not one single thing against any Roman Catholic," but the peril facing the nation was real. "I am definitely opposed to everything Roman Catholicism stands for, especially its position relative to religious freedom and church and state. It is our desire to direct the minds and the thoughts of our readers in a channel opposing Roman Catholicism." The editor concluded that, although he was a Democrat, "I serve notice that I will not vote for a Roman Catholic." Elsewhere in the same issue, another writer announced, "I would no sooner vote for a Roman Catholic than for a communist."[21]

---

20. Tract, "The Enemy Within Our Borders, compiled by A Converted Roman Catholic Priest," published by Prayer Sanctuary, Minneapolis, Minnesota, "Catholic Issue" folder, Pre-Presidential Papers, 1960 Campaign, Box 1044, John F. Kennedy Library.

21. Editor's note, "The Roman Catholic Issue," *The Baptist Examiner* (Russell, Kentucky), May 7, 1960, 1; Bob L. Ross, "Why I Would Not Vote for a Roman Catholic Candidate," *The Baptist Examiner* (Russell, Kentucky), May 7, 1960, 3.

The number of anti-Catholic tracts, however, was probably fewer than the number of anti-Catholic sermons. On July 3, 1960, for instance, W. A. Criswell, pastor of the First Baptist Church in Dallas, Texas, warned his auditors that "Roman Catholicism is not only a religion, it is a political tyranny."[22]

By mid-summer, after Kennedy had secured the Democratic nomination at the convention in Los Angeles, worried dispatches from the heartland began to filter in to Kennedy campaign headquarters. "May I have your urgent attention for the problem of religion in the farm belt," John Kenneth Galbraith, the Harvard economist, wrote in a confidential memorandum to Kennedy. "Religion in the rural corn belt, Great Plains and down into rural Texas has become an issue greater than either income or peace," he warned. "One of the problems in Iowa and the surrounding states is that local leaders in thought and ideas are not yet actively combatting the tendency to decide the issue on religious grounds," Galbraith continued. "They are the people who must say that to allow religion to enter the decision is to decide for reaction." Noting that "religious prejudice is a stalking horse for reaction, a diversion from the real and important issues," Galbraith echoed the advice from his fellow Harvard professor Archibald Cox earlier in the campaign. He urged Kennedy to address the religion issue directly and to solicit strongly worded endorsements "from Protestant liberals and scholars who are known to know and respect you," adding that "the fact remains that where prospects are bright, as say Minnesota, Michigan or (less certainly) Wisconsin,

---

22. Quoted in Chandler Davidson, *Race and Class in Texas Politics* (Princeton, NJ: Princeton University Press, 1990), 214.

it is partly because you have articulate liberals in power and making your case."[23]

In assessing the progress of the campaign in mid-August, Theodore Sorensen was generally positive, though he continued to worry about the religion issue. "Given the normal Democratic majority, and assuming that his personal appeal, hard work, and political organization produce as before, Senator Kennedy will win in November unless defeated by the religious issue," Sorensen wrote in an internal memorandum. "This makes neutralization of this issue the key to the election." He advocated the formation of "national, state and local committees of leading Protestants, both lay and clergy, willing to attack this issue and work with and through state and local council of churches and ministerial associations."[24]

Kennedy was not without defenders. "The danger facing us is not, as some would have us believe, a religious hierarchy," the Episcopal bishop for the Diocese of Pittsburgh wrote. "It is the hierarchy of suspicion, fear and bigotry that is really dangerous." James A. Pike, bishop of the Episcopal Diocese of California, deplored the circulation of what he called "hate literature" targeted against Kennedy and the Roman Catholic Church. The attempt, he said, "to seek to persuade citizens that they should in no wise vote for a man simply because he is Roman Catholic is outright bigotry and is a violation of the spirit of the constitutional prohibition of a religious test for public office." Speaking at the Michigan

23. Letter, John Kenneth Galbraith to John F. Kennedy, August 25, 1960, "Religious Issue" folder, Pre-Presidential Papers, 1960 Campaign, Box 993, John F. Kennedy Library.

24. Memorandum on the Religious Issue, Theodore C. Sorenson, August 15, 1960, "Religious Issue: Campaign Material" folder 2, Theodore C. Sorenson Papers, Campaign Files, 1959–60, Box 25, John F. Kennedy Library.

State Fair, Pike called on Christians "of whatever denomination" to "vigorously deplore and earnestly seek to counteract this rising tide of 'hate' literature in our midst."[25]

A newspaper in Kansas, a state not known for its Roman Catholic population, also defended Kennedy. "Much of the campaign against Catholicism is filthy slander, the product of diseased minds," the *Wichita Beacon* opined on August 26, 1960, just as the fall campaign lurched into motion. The editorial, entitled "Let's Play Fair with Catholics," urged responsible Americans to "protest against vicious lies and outrageous attacks on the character and loyalty of a large segment of American society" and noted that "Catholic people generally measure up at least as well as Protestants in matters of morality, patriotism and good-neighborliness." The editorial concluded with an appeal to Protestant leaders. "Protestants of the decent sort owe it to themselves to challenge all immoderate and vehement statements against the Catholics. And when the statements have the purpose of inciting hatred and violence there is nothing to do but turn away from the hater."[26]

A group of Protestant leaders, however, those of the putatively responsible sort to which the *Wichita Beacon* appealed, sought unabashedly to derail Kennedy's candidacy. And their opposition posed a greater, more credible threat than the scurrilous anti-Catholic literature flooding the electorate. Norman Vincent

---

25. Statement of the Episcopal Bishop of the Diocese of Pittsburgh, "Religion" folder, Pre-Presidential Papers, 1960 Campaign, Box 1049, John F. Kennedy Library; "Pike Denounces Campaign 'Hate,'" *New York Times,* September 5, 1960.

26. "Let's Play Fair with Catholics," *Wichita Beacon,* August 26, 1960.

Peale, pastor of Marble Collegiate Church in New York City, fired the opening salvo just days after the West Virginia primary, when Kennedy mistakenly—hopefully—declared that his victory had "buried the religious issue once and for all." Peale released to the press a letter he had written to Robert Kennedy, the candidate's brother and campaign manager, quibbling with his use of language. "I hope you won't mind if I respectfully call your attention to the implication of superiority in your use of terms," the minister said. "By the phrase 'non-Catholic' it seems to me that you are actually deprecating the majority of people in this country." Peale concluded: "I wonder how you might react to the term 'non-Protestant' as designating members of your Roman Catholic Church?"[27]

Peale, unabashedly partisan on behalf of Richard Nixon, the Republican nominee, was just getting started, and he enjoyed the cooperation of several other Protestant leaders, including Billy Graham, another Nixon loyalist. Donald Gill, a Baptist minister, took a leave of absence from his position as assistant secretary for public affairs at the National Association of Evangelicals to head a group that sought to raise questions about the suitability of a Roman Catholic as president. Graham convened a meeting of approximately thirty Protestant leaders in Montreux, Switzerland, on August 18, 1960, in order to strategize against Kennedy.[28]

Peale was present, as was Harold Ockenga, pastor of Park Street Congregational Church in Boston and president of Fuller

---

27. "A Kennedy Irks Peale," New York Times, May 21, 1960.

28. Graham recounts his involvement with these activities in his autobiography, Just As I Am: The Autobiography of Billy Graham (San Francisco: HarperOne, 1997), 391–92.

Theological Seminary, and L. Nelson Bell, Graham's father-in-law and an editor of *Christianity Today*. The proceedings are still shrouded in secrecy, and the only solid evidence survives in a letter from Ruth Peale, wife of the Marble Collegiate minister. "Norman had a conference yesterday at Montreux, Switzerland," the letter reads. "They were unanimous in feeling that the Protestants in America must be aroused in some way, or the solid block Catholic voting, plus money, will take this election."[29]

The Protestants gathered in Switzerland decided to set up a meeting with Nixon and then to organize a forum to address the religious issue. Peale, the most prominent person in the group, headed the meeting, which took place on Wednesday, September 7, two days after Labor Day, the traditional start of the fall campaign. The venue was the Mayflower Hotel in Washington, the same place, paradoxically, where members of the Fair Campaign Practices Committee had met in March to issue a statement calling for religious toleration. Despite Peale's public protestations—"As a Protestant minister I would be recreant if I told people how to vote," he said—the statement coming out of the September meeting, adopted unanimously, declared that Kennedy's Catholicism was a "major factor" in the presidential campaign and that a Roman Catholic president would face "extreme pressure from the hierarchy of his church." The Mayflower gathering, which became known almost immediately as the "Peale group," decided

---

29. The Montreux meeting was discovered by historian Carol V. R. George; see *God's Salesman: Norman Vincent Peale and the Power of Positive Thinking* (New York: Oxford University Press, 1993), 200. An excerpt from Ruth Peale's letter is quoted in Alva James, "Leaders Mixed State, Religion," *Syracuse* (NY) *Post-Standard,* December 7, 1992.

to organize as the National Conference of Citizens for Religious Freedom.[30]

Peale characterized the meeting of 150 Protestant leaders at the Mayflower Hotel as "more or less representative of the evangelical, conservative Protestants." The statement noted that the Catholic Church "is a political as well as a religious organization" which had "repeatedly attempted to break down the wall of separation between church and state." Harold Ockenga, standing along side of Peale at the news conference, suggested that Kennedy's repeated affirmations of the separation of church and state should be discounted, comparing them to the statements of Nikita Khrushchev, the Soviet premier, regarding world peace. Like Khrushchev, Ockenga said, Kennedy is "a captive of a system." Finally, when asked if the gathering had discussed how Nixon's Quaker faith affected his policies, Peale allowed that "I don't know that he ever let it bother him."[31]

Graham's role in organizing the Washington meeting, having earlier convened the smaller group in Montreux, belied the assurances he had given Kennedy just days before the August 18 strategy session in Switzerland. "There is a rumor circulating in the Democratic Party that I intend to raise the religious issue publicly during the presidential campaign," Graham wrote to Kennedy on August 10. "This is not true. In fact, I would like to commend you for facing it squarely and courageously." Graham

30. "Peale to Head Protestant Forum on Religious Issue in Campaign," *New York Times,* September 4, 1960; Peter Braestrup, "Protestant Unit Wary on Kennedy," *New York Times,* September 8, 1960.

31. Braestrup, "Protestant Unit"; quoted in Sorensen, *Kennedy,* 188; "Religious Issue Stirs Controversy," *New York Times,* September 11, 1960.

went on to concede that "I shall probably vote for Vice President Nixon for several reasons, including a long-standing personal friendship. I am sure you can understand my position." He closed the letter, which he hoped would remain confidential, by assuring Kennedy of his support should the Democratic nominee win the election: "I will do all in my power to help unify the American people behind you."[32]

I will leave it to others to judge whether Graham was being disingenuous. He had forged a friendship with Nixon during the previous decade when both men were anti-communist crusaders, and few Americans doubted his support for Nixon. Later in the campaign, Graham visited Henry Luce at the Time & Life Building and, according to his autobiography, said, "I want to help Nixon without blatantly endorsing him." Graham drafted an article praising Nixon that stopped just short of a full endorsement. Luce was prepared to run it in *Time* magazine but pulled it at the last minute. Still, the fact that Graham was working behind the scenes effectively to discredit Kennedy's candidacy because of his faith, notwithstanding his protestations to the Democratic candidate, appears to contradict the spirit, if not the letter, of Graham's assurances.[33]

Because Graham remained in the background, however, Peale took a great deal of criticism for the gathering in Washington and the statement calling Kennedy's fitness for office into question. The blatant excesses of the statement from the "Peale group" may have

---

32. Letter, Billy Graham to John F. Kennedy, August 10, 1960, "Religion" folder, Pre-Presidential Papers, Senate Files, Box 550, John F. Kennedy Library.

33. Graham, *Just As I Am,* 392–99. Graham claims to have been relieved that Luce pulled the article.

played out to Kennedy's advantage by stirring a reaction. The editor of the *Saturday Evening Post,* a Nixon supporter, said that he was "deeply disturbed" by the Washington gathering. "Dr. Peale and his collaborators have rendered our country a disservice in giving the religious issue a respectable front," Lewis I. Newman, a rabbi on the Upper West Side of Manhattan, declared. "The Protestant statement is a bald and unashamed bid for the election of the candidate of a political party." A rabbi from the Bronx compared the sentiments behind the statement to apartheid in South Africa and segregation in the South. Israel Goldstein, rabbi at B'nai Jeshurun in Manhattan, said, "It is disturbing to see that there are sections of American public opinion which in effect are saying that a Catholic must never be President."[34]

John C. Bennett, president of Union Theological Seminary in New York City, and Reinhold Niebuhr, also of Union, accused the "Peale group" of "blind prejudice." Bennett attributed the statement to "a kind of Protestant underworld" and declared that voting against a candidate because of his faith was "bad politics and worse religion." Bennett noted the partisanship of both Peale and the entire Washington gathering; they would never support a liberal Democrat, Bennett insisted, "no matter what his religion." *World Outlook* magazine, a Methodist publication, wondered why the Protestant group didn't grill Nixon on how historical Quaker commitments to pacifism might influence his foreign policy. The *Catholic Courier-Journal,* the official publication of the Diocese of Rochester, New York, also weighed in on the matter. "The fact that anti-Catholic bias is rampant in Southern states comes hardly as a surprise," the

---

34. George, *God's Salesman,* 206; "3 Rabbis Assail Electoral Bias," *New York Times,* September 11, 1960.

paper said, "but when men of the caliber of Dr. Norman Vincent Peale join the prejudiced ranks then we are not only surprised we are also deeply disappointed."[35]

Peale, stung by the criticism, severed his ties with the National Conference of Citizens for Religious Freedom and went into hiding. He protested that he did not convene the Washington meeting, but that he was merely an observer whose role was "relatively minor," a fine point lost on the media but confirmed by other insiders, including (much later) Billy Graham. The *Philadelphia Inquirer*, published by Peale's friend Walter Annenberg, dropped his syndicated column, "Confident Living," as did the *Pittsburgh Press* and other newspapers around the country. Senator Henry "Scoop" Jackson of Washington, chair of the Democratic National Committee, suggested that the title of Peale's famous book, *The Power of Positive Thinking,* should be changed to *The Power of Positive Prejudice.* When Peale emerged from seclusion, recognizing that his reputation had been badly damaged by his association with such a blatantly partisan group, he submitted a letter of resignation to his New York congregation. The church refused to consider it.[36]

---

35. Quoted in George, *God's Salesman,* 202; "'Protestant Underworld' Cited as Source of Attack on Kennedy," *New York Times,* September 11, 1960.

36. "Ends Tie to Protestants Who Doubted Kennedy Could Resist Vatican," *New York Times,* September 16, 1960; George, *God's Salesman,* 206; Tom Wicker, "Jackson Urges a Press Inquiry on 'Organized' Hate Campaign," *New York Times,* September 15, 1960. In his autobiography, Graham acknowledges that Peale took a disproportionate amount of blame for the Mayflower meeting and said that he later apologized to Peale for letting him twist in the wind. Graham remained unscathed, even though the gathering in Montreux, which he had convened, laid the groundwork. See Graham, *Just As I Am,* 392. About the Washington meeting, Graham writes: "I encouraged Peale to go, privately glad that I would still be in Europe and therefore unable to attend" (Graham, *Just As I Am,* 392).

*  *  *

In the Kennedy camp, the statement emanating from the "Peale group" prodded them to action. Kennedy himself, though he hoped that the West Virginia primary had laid the religious issue to rest, predicted that "it will come on the stage again." Peale and his confreres had brought it to center stage. Kennedy reluctantly accepted an invitation to address the matter before the Ministerial Association in Houston on September 12, just five days after the Mayflower meeting. During the previous weekend, while campaigning in Los Angeles, the candidate had worked on his speech together with Sorensen, who remarked to a friend, "We can win or lose the election right there in Houston on Monday night."[37]

Three hundred ministers gathered in the pink-and-green-carpeted Crystal Ballroom, along with an equal number of observers. The candidate, seated next to the Presbyterian minister who chaired the group, fidgeted almost imperceptibly, waiting for the lights of the television cameras to blink on at nine o'clock. Earlier in the day, while campaigning in San Antonio, Kennedy and Johnson had encountered pickets that read: "We Want the Bible and the Constitution" and "We Don't Want the Kremlin or the Vatican."[38]

Kennedy strode to the podium. "I am not the Catholic candidate for president," he insisted. "I am the Democratic Party's candidate for president, who happens also to be a Catholic." The

---

37. Quoted in Sorensen, *Kennedy,* 175; quoted in White, *Making of the President 1960,* 260.

38. Merle Miller, *Lyndon: An Oral Biography* (New York: G. P. Putnam's Sons, 1980), 265.

issue at stake, he said, is "not what kind of church I believe in, for that should be important only to me, but what kind of America I believe in." I believe in an America, the Democratic nominee said, "where no man is denied public office merely because his religion differs from the president who might appoint him or the people who might elect him." Kennedy declared that the presidency "is a great office that must be neither humbled by making it the instrument of any religious group, nor tarnished by arbitrarily withholding its occupancy from the members of any religious group." He argued for a president "whose views on religion are his own private affair, neither imposed on him by the nation or imposed upon him as a condition to holding that office."[39]

Kennedy's speech was being televised live on twenty-two stations throughout Texas, and he sought to clinch his argument with a local reference. He cited his own distinguished military service in World War II and noted that there was "no religious test" at the Battle of the Alamo: "For side by side with Bowie and Crockett died Fuentes and McCafferty and Bailey and Bedillio and Carey—but no one knows whether they were Catholics or not." The audience of Protestant ministers, restive and suspicious at the beginning of the speech, remained silent throughout the eleven-minute address. Kennedy expressed his hope that he would be judged by his qualifications for office and by his policies, not by his faith. If the 1960 presidential election, he said, "is decided on the basis that forty million Americans lost their chance of being

---

39. Gladwin Hill, "Reaction of Ministers," *New York Times*, September 14, 1960. Kennedy's speech at the Rice Hotel has been reprinted often and is widely available. One source for the text is White, *Making of the President 1960*, Appendix C. It also appears in this book as Appendix 1.

president on the day they were baptized, then it is the whole nation that will be the loser in the eyes of Catholics and non-Catholics around the world, in the eyes of history, and in the eyes of our own people."[40]

Theodore Sorensen judged Kennedy's speech at the Rice Hotel "the best speech of his campaign and one of the most important in his life," surpassed only by his inaugural address four months later. Kennedy took questions from the audience, some of them hostile; several of the acrimonious exchanges, according to the *New York Times,* were prompted by conservative ministers who generally shunned the meetings of the Ministerial Association. Kennedy, however, handled them with grace, wit, and aplomb. Then he concluded:

> Let me finally say that I am delighted to come here today. I don't want anyone to think, because they interrogate me on this important question, that I regard that as unfair or unreasonable or that somebody who is concerned about the matter is prejudiced or bigoted.
>
> I think religion is basic in the establishment of the American system, and, therefore, any candidate for the office, I think, should submit himself to the questions of any reasonable man.
>
> My only limit would be that if somebody said, "Regardless of Senator Kennedy's position, regardless of how much evidence he has given that what he says he means,

---

40. Gladwin Hill, "Reaction of Ministers," *New York Times,* September 14, 1960. Quotations from speech are taken from White, *Making of the President 1960,* Appendix C.

I still won't vote for him because he is a member of that church."

I would consider that unreasonable. What I consider to be reasonable in an exercise of free will and free choice is to ask Senator Kennedy to state his views as broadly as possible. Investigate his record to see whether he states what he believes and then make an independent and rational judgment as to whether he could be entrusted with this highly important position.

So I want you to know that I am grateful to you for inviting me tonight. I am sure that I have made no converts to my church, but I do hope that, at least, my view, which I believe to be the view of my fellow Catholics who hold office, I hope that it may be of some value in at least assisting you to make a careful judgment.

The campaign thought that the senator's performance had been so effective that they published transcripts and produced a thirty-minute film for distribution beyond Texas in an effort finally to quell the so-called religious issue. Even Sam Rayburn, speaker of the House of Representatives, offered his assessment of Kennedy's appearance in Houston. "As we say in my part of Texas," Rayburn drawled, "he ate 'em blood raw."[41]

---

41. Sorensen, *Kennedy*, 190; Hill, "Reaction of Ministers," *New York Times*, September 14, 1960; Transcript, September 12, 1960, "Religion" folder, Pre-Presidential Papers, 1960 Campaign, Box 1049, John F. Kennedy Library; Memorandum, James Wine to John Siegenthaler, October 5, 1960, "Religious Issue: Correspondence" folder, Robert F. Kennedy Papers, Pre-Administration Political Files, General Subject Files, 1959–60, Box 47, John F. Kennedy Library; quoted in Boller, *Presidential Campaigns*, 298.

The issue refused entirely to die. Although an array of religious leaders, including Protestants, hailed Kennedy's speech—one erstwhile critic conceded that Kennedy had "lifted himself above that issue"—others stepped up their criticisms. "No matter what Kennedy might say, he cannot separate himself from his church if he is a true Catholic," Ramsey Pollard, president of the Southern Baptist Convention, declared. "All we ask is that Roman Catholicism lift its bloody hand from the throats of those that want to worship in the church of their choice." Pollard, protesting that he was not a bigot, boasted that his church "has enough members to beat Kennedy in this area if they all vote like I tell them to."[42]

Another Southern Baptist, W. A. Criswell, pastor of First Baptist Church in Dallas, persisted in his crusade against Kennedy. "It is written in our country's constitution that church and state must be, in this nation, forever separate and free," Criswell wrote in a publication called *United Evangelical Action*. Religious faith, the redoubtable fundamentalist declared, must be voluntary, and "in the very nature of the case, there can be no proper union of church and state." K. Owen White, pastor of First Baptist Church in downtown Houston, credited Kennedy with being "forthright and frank" in his speech to the Ministerial Association, but he continued to object to a Roman Catholic as president because the church requires its members "to take positions on public matters." The Permian Basin Baptist Association, in West Texas, responded to Kennedy's speech in Houston with a resolution charging that

---

42. Charles Grutzner, "Poling Praises Kennedy's Stand on Religion Issue," *New York Times,* September 14, 1960; quoted in Sorensen, *Kennedy,* 194.

the Democratic candidate was "either denying the teaching of his church or is seeking to delude the American people."[43]

Some of the Baptist opposition to Kennedy was thoughtful. "I am not opposed to Catholicism as such, but to the clerical control of most of the Catholic people," E. S. James, editor of the *Baptist Standard,* wrote to the candidate. "To me, government is a moral matter, and any administrator of government would be guided in a large measure by his interpretation of the moral issues. Therefore, I cannot see how it would be possible under the present clerical system of Roman Catholicism for any man to be faithful to those tenets of the Catholic church and still be absolutely free to exercise his own judgment rather than the judgment of the hierarchy in his church."[44]

The opposition to a Roman Catholic candidate on the part of Baptist clergy was not entirely without warrant, even though the criticism frequently edged into the realm of prejudice rather than principle. The two hallmarks of Baptist belief are adult, or believer's, baptism (as opposed to infant baptism) and the notion of liberty of conscience and the separation of church and state. These ideas can be traced to Roger Williams, the founder of the Baptist

43. W. A. Criswell, "Religious Freedom and the Presidency," *United Evangelical Action* 19 (September 1960), 9–10; quoted in Hill, "Reaction of Ministers," *New York Times,* September 14, 1960; "West Texas Baptist Criticizes Kennedy," *New York Times,* September 15, 1960.

44. Letter, E. S. James (editor, *Baptist Standard*) to John F. Kennedy, March 11, 1960, "Religious Issue: Campaign Material" folder 2, Theodore C. Sorenson Papers, Campaign Files, 1959–60, Box 25, John F. Kennedy Library.

tradition in America. Williams came to the New World in 1631 as pastor of the Puritan congregation in Salem, Massachusetts. Very quickly, however, he ran afoul of the Puritan authorities in the colony because he warned of the dangers of conflating church and state. Williams wanted to protect what he called the "garden of the church" from contamination by the "wilderness of the world," and he sought to do so by means of (again, his words) a "wall of separation."

This notion that church and state should function as separate entities was a new idea, one that the Puritans, in their impulse to form a theocratic order in Massachusetts, regarded with utmost suspicion. Williams was expelled from the colony, whereupon he went to what became Rhode Island and founded there both the Baptist tradition in America as well as a colony that enshrined his ideas of liberty of individual conscience and the separation of church and state. Throughout American history—until the rise of the Religious Right in the late 1970s—Baptists have been guardians on this wall of separation between church and state. From Williams himself in the seventeenth century to John Leland and Isaac Backus in the eighteenth century to George Washington Truett and W. A. Criswell in the twentieth century, Baptists have fervently believed that religion functions best apart from entanglements with the government.

Baptists have stoutly defended the First Amendment, especially the disestablishment clause: "Congress shall make no law respecting an establishment of religion." The Baptist objections to Kennedy's candidacy, therefore, cannot be dismissed simply as religious bigotry. To the extent that Criswell and others actually believed that Kennedy's election represented a threat to the First Amendment—a not wholly unreasonable position, given the history of Roman Catholicism in Europe—they were expressing legitimate concerns.

Whether the articulation of those principles served really as a proxy for anti-Catholic or anti-liberal or anti-Democratic sentiment, on the other hand, remains difficult to determine, especially at a remove of several decades. The fact that Criswell (among many other Baptists) abandoned the Baptist principle of church-state separation in his embrace of Ronald Reagan in the 1980s—on August 24, 1984, during the Republican National Convention, Criswell declared: "I believe this notion of the separation of church and state was the figment of some infidel's imagination"—Criswell's inconsistency calls into question his motives during the 1960 campaign. But that judgment reads history retroactively and for that reason probably is not entirely fair.[45]

Not all Baptists opposed Kennedy. "There are many valid issues upon which the forthcoming Presidential campaign should be waged," the *Crusader,* a magazine published by the American Baptist Convention, declared, "but voting for or against a candidate on the basis of his religious affiliation is not one of them."[46]

J. H. Jackson, president of the National Baptist Convention, the largest denomination of African American Baptists, sent an open letter to Billy Graham in response to an article Graham had written entitled "Graham Predicts Religion at Polls." "You

45. Quoted in Richard V. Pierard, "Religion and the 1984 Election Campaign," *Review of Religious Research* 27 (December 1985), 104–5.

46. "The Religious 'Issue' in the Presidential Campaign," circular "Authorized and paid for by the District of Columbia Committee for John F. Kennedy," John F. Kennedy Library.

make a sweeping judgment about the Catholic Church and then jump to the conclusion regarding the fitness of an American to be president of these United States," Jackson admonished his Baptist brother. "The American people are not planning to elect a Catholic for the president of the United States. They are planning to elect an American citizen. It matters not what his religion might be." While professing respect for Graham, Jackson continued: "We should urge the American people to rise above prejudices of every kind and go to the polls in November and vote as Americans for an American to be president of Americans." Finally, Jackson appealed to quintessential Baptist principles: "If religion is present at the polls in November I hope it will be an inclusive religion that embraces the fact of the brotherhood of man and the fatherhood of God, and then leaves every particular denomination and group to choose his own theology, his own ritual, and his own form of church government."[47]

As the presidential campaign of 1960 wound down, the religious issue persisted. Henry Jackson, head of the Democratic Party, called on Nixon "to repudiate Dr. Peale and his group by name." Adlai Stevenson, the Democratic presidential nominee in both 1952 and 1956, also called on Nixon to disassociate himself from Peale. Harry Truman, the Democratic former president, charged that, in his hometown of Independence, Missouri, "the Republicans are sending out all the dirty pamphlets they

47. Open letter, J. H. Jackson (president, National Baptist Convention) to Billy Graham, August 25, 1960, "Religion" folder, Pre-Presidential Papers, Senate Files, Box 550, John F. Kennedy Library.

can find on the religious issue," though he exonerated Nixon himself.[48]

Intelligence coming into the campaign headquarters from around the country reported "a serious intensification of distribution of anti-Catholic literature." "Tracts against Catholics, and against the election of a Catholic President, are flooding into Central Ohio, delivered by mail, and door-to-door," the co-chair of Ohio Citizens for Kennedy reported to Robert Kennedy on October 29. "Tomorrow a number of Protestant fundamentalist churches are celebrating 'Reformation Sunday' with sermons on such topics as 'God's choice for President.'" The correspondent characterized the situation in Ohio as "nasty."[49]

Campaign strategists recognized that they had no chance of swaying hard-bitten anti-Catholics. But they sought some way to turn the bigotry to their advantage among more reasonable voters. "If these people can be made aware that there *is* a mammoth, vicious anti-Catholic drive underway, that the forces of bigotry and prejudice *are* working ceaselessly to prevent the election of JFK," an internal campaign memorandum read, "that the appeals made by the anti-Catholic forces are distorted, inaccurate and

---

48. Tom Wicker, "Jackson Urges a Press Inquiry on 'Organized' Hate Campaign," *New York Times,* September 15, 1960; John Wicklein, "Niebuhr and Bennett Say Raising of Religious Issue Spurs Bigotry," *New York Times,* September 16, 1960; "Truman Hails Nixon on Religious Issue," *New York Times,* September 15, 1960.

49. Memorandum on the Religious Issue [author unknown], October 20, 1960, "Religious Issue: Correspondence" folder, Robert F. Kennedy Papers, Pre-Administration Political Files, General Subject Files, 1959–60, Box 47, John F. Kennedy Library; Memorandum, Mrs. Robert A. Rennie (co-chair, Ohio Citizens for Kennedy) to Robert F. Kennedy, October 29, 1960, "Religious Issue: Correspondence" folder, Robert F. Kennedy Papers, Pre-Administration Political Files, General Subject Files, 1959–60, Box 47, John F. Kennedy Library.

scurrilous, and that JFK *is* in danger of losing several states not because of his position on the issues, not because of his ability, not because of his program, but merely because he is a Catholic, then there is a real possibility of winning some of these votes."[50]

The voting on November 8, 1960, produced one of the closest elections in American history. Kennedy won 49.7 percent of the popular vote to Nixon's 49.5 percent. Kennedy's election finally laid to rest the notion that a Roman Catholic could never be elected president of the United States. The 1960 election also represented an almost eerie reversal of the 1928 campaign, when Alfred E. Smith, a Roman Catholic, lost to Herbert Hoover, who became America's first Quaker president. In 1960, however, the Roman Catholic prevailed over the Quaker, Richard Nixon—who also happened to be Hoover's eighth cousin, once removed. The victory of a Quaker over a Roman Catholic in 1928 produced the first Quaker president in American history; the triumph of a Roman Catholic over a Quaker in 1960 produced the first Roman Catholic president.[51]

Historians and political scientists have attributed Kennedy's victory to several factors: Kennedy's superior performance in the televised debates, especially the first debate in Chicago; Nixon's

*[margin handwriting: Why JFK won]*

50. Memorandum on the Religious Issue [author unknown], October 20, 1960, "Religious Issue: Correspondence" folder, Robert F. Kennedy Papers, Pre-Administration Political Files, General Subject Files, 1959–60, Box 47, John F. Kennedy Library.

51. Regarding Nixon's relationship to Hoover, see William A. DeGregorio, *The Complete Book of U.S. Presidents: From George Washington to George W. Bush,* rev. ed. (New York: Barnes & Noble Books, 2002), 464.

brief hospitalization, which sidelined him during a crucial juncture of the campaign; popular weariness with the Eisenhower-Nixon years; even the conspiracy theory that Richard J. Daley, mayor of Chicago, stole the election for Kennedy. All of these variables (with the possible exception of the latter) doubtless played a role. But religion also was a factor. Although Reinhold Niebuhr and John Bennett of Union Seminary declared that the statement emanating from the "Peale group" had "loosed the floodgates of religious bigotry," the overall effect was quite the opposite. Peale and his Protestant colleagues at the Washington gathering created a backlash of sympathy for the Democratic nominee, which had the effect of silencing his most credible religious critics, thereby minimizing the issue.[52]

Finally, in a twist of irony, it may have been a Baptist who provided the critical margin in Kennedy's favor. On October 19, two days before the final Nixon-Kennedy debate, Martin Luther King Jr. was arrested in Atlanta for trying to desegregate a restaurant. He was sentenced to four months of hard labor and taken, under cover of darkness, to the state prison in Reidsville. Coretta, King's wife, was six months pregnant and frantic about her husband's safety as a black man in a distant prison. She called Harris Wofford, one of Kennedy's campaign aides, and sought his help. Wofford went over the head of Robert Kennedy, the campaign manager, and pleaded with Sargent Shriver to ask the candidate to place a phone call to Coretta. "That's a wonderful idea," Kennedy said.[53]

---

52. Quoted in Wicklein, "Niebuhr and Bennett."

53. Quoted in David J. Garrow, *Bearing the Cross: Martin Luther King, Jr., and the Southern Christian Leadership Conference* (New York: William Morrow, 1986), 147.

The brief phone conversation had the immediate effect of reassuring King's wife, but the ripple effects arguably swept the Democrat into office as news of Kennedy's gesture of support spread rapidly through the African American community. Robert Kennedy was initially miffed at Wofford's actions (and told him so), fearful that alignment with the civil-rights activist would jeopardize Kennedy's standing with white Southerners. But, on reflection, Robert Kennedy sought to intercede with the judge on King's behalf. After his phone call, the judge agreed to King's release on bond. When the civil-rights leader arrived at the airport, back from incarceration, he declared that he was "deeply indebted to Senator Kennedy."[54]

King's father, Martin Luther King Sr., was even more effusive. The elder King, senior pastor at Ebenezer Baptist Church, had been leaning toward Nixon in the 1960 campaign, in part because of Kennedy's religion. But the Democratic candidate's phone call changed his mind. "Because this man was willing to wipe the tears from my daughter-in-law's eyes," he declared, "I've got a suitcase of votes, and I'm going to take them to Mr. Kennedy and dump them in his lap."[55]

Kennedy's determination to bracket religious affiliation from political considerations was compelling to just enough Americans to allow him to squeak into office and thereby to

54. Quoted in Garrow, *Bearing the Cross,* 148.

55. Quoted in Boller, *Presidential Campaigns,* 300. For Coretta's account of the Kennedy phone call and its repercussions, see Coretta Scott King, *My Life with Martin Luther King, Jr.* (New York: Holt, Rinehart & Winston, 1969), 195–97. When told of the elder King's comment about Catholicism, Kennedy quipped: "Imagine Martin Luther King having a bigot for a father." Then, after a pause: "Well, we all have fathers, don't we?" Quoted in King, *My Life,* 195–97.

demolish the shibboleth that no Roman Catholic could ever be president. Prejudicial statements against Catholics, however, did not disappear altogether. In 1962, for instance, a graduate of Princeton Theological Seminary who identified himself as an evangelical, Loraine Boettner, published a tome of nearly five hundred pages called *Roman Catholicism,* which warned about "the advances that Romanism is making today in this nation and in other parts of the world." Boettner drew a distinction between Christianity and Roman Catholicism and asserted that "American freedoms are being threatened today by two totalitarian systems, Communism and Roman Catholicism." Boettner's anti-Catholic screed, appearing as it did following Kennedy's election and prior to his assassination, played to lingering nativist fears. In the United States, he warned, "Romanism is growing faster than is Communism and is the more dangerous since it covers its real nature with a cloak of religion."[56]

Boettner's *Roman Catholicism* provided a theological gloss to Paul Blanshard's earlier warnings about the threat posed by Catholicism to America's freedoms. And it supplied incontrovertible evidence that, despite Kennedy's election, anti-Catholic sentiments still found a hearing among some Americans. The overwhelming public grief surrounding the death of the young president finally, albeit temporarily, stilled those voices.

In mid-January 1960, just days before Kennedy's inauguration, Billy Graham had called on the president-elect in Palm Beach,

---

56. Loraine Boettner, *Roman Catholicism* (Philadelphia: Presbyterian and Reformed Publishing Co., 1962), 2, 3.

Florida, for lunch and a round of golf. "I believe President Kennedy will become the most prayed-for man in the world," Graham told a press conference at the Washington Hotel in Palm Beach. The evangelist suggested that Kennedy's victory had demonstrated that there was less religious prejudice among American voters than many had feared. He ventured that the outcome of the 1960 presidential campaign may have diminished forever the importance of religion in American elections.[57]

Graham, as it turned out, was only partially prescient. Kennedy's election did indeed silence—or at least muffle—the strident voices of anti-Catholicism in American society, the naysayers who insisted that a Roman Catholic could never rise to the presidency. Kennedy's persuasive argument in the course of the 1960 campaign that religion should not play a role in political considerations, coupled with the overreaching of the "Peale group," ushered in an era during which matters of faith had little bearing on presidential politics or political decision-making. Ironically, it was the morally bankrupt presidency of Graham's friend, the man whom Kennedy defeated in 1960, that set the stage for a reinsertion of faith and religious sentiment into presidential politics.

---

57. "Dr. Graham Says Election Aids Church Unity," *New York Times,* January 17, 1961.

Lyndon Johnson, a member of the Disciples of Christ, was not demonstrably pious. His ethic of the stronger taking responsibility for the weaker, however, informed both his domestic Great Society ambitions as well as, tragically, his prosecution of the war in Vietnam.

Billy Graham and Richard Nixon forged a friendship in the early 1950s that weathered the various scandals that marked Nixon's checkered career. Graham detected vast reservoirs of piety in his friend that generally escaped the notice of others.

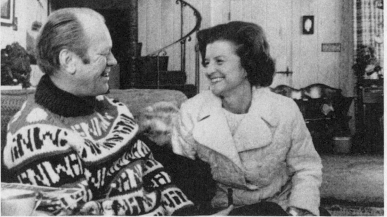

Gerald and Betty Ford in their home in Vail, Colorado, in December 1974. Ford, the only president in American history never to have been elected either president or vice president, issued a preemptive pardon of Richard Nixon, his predecessor, only a month after taking office on August 9, 1974.

TWO

# DO UNTO OTHERS

*Lyndon B. Johnson, Richard Nixon, and the Improbable Presidency of Gerald R. Ford*

The lore surrounding Lyndon B. Johnson is rich and descriptive and, some of it perhaps, apocryphal. One story has it that Johnson, a larger-than-life figure, asked one of his assistants, Bill Moyers, a Baptist minister, to offer grace before a meal at the White House. As Moyers, sitting at the opposite end of the table, began praying, Johnson bellowed, "Speak up, Moyers, I can't hear you."

The young assistant responded in a quiet, even voice, "I wasn't talking to you, sir."[1]

Lyndon Johnson, an enigmatic character of Shakespearean dimensions, was born into poverty in a three-room farmhouse along the Pedernales River, near Johnson City, Texas. Unlike John Kennedy, who had a clear religious lineage, Johnson's was

---

1. I sent an early draft of this chapter to Bill Moyers, who was kind enough to read it—and to confirm that this story is true. E-mail correspondence from Bill Moyers to Randall Balmer, March 4, 2007.

a mixture of various influences, from Baptist to Christadelphian. Rebekah, Lyndon's mother, was a prim Baptist, but his father's religious commitments ranged from diffuse to nonexistent and included a sometime interest in the Christadelphians, a marginal, non-trinitarian group with roots in nineteenth-century Britain and America. "Though not exactly an atheist or agnostic he never seemed to give much thought to formal religion," Sam Houston Johnson, Lyndon's brother, said about their father, Sam Ealy Johnson. "Still, he was deeply committed to certain ideas that you might consider religious. He was certainly a believer in the dignity of all human beings regardless of race or creed, and some of that rubbed off on all of us."[2]

Lyndon Johnson himself chose still another route, the precise explanation for which is lost in the mists of history. At age fifteen he joined the Christian Church (Disciples of Christ), a Protestant group with roots in the Restorationist movement of the early nineteenth century, an attempt to restore Christianity to its primitive, first-century purity. The attraction for Johnson may have been a girlfriend who was associated with the movement. Or it may have been the influence of his cousins, Margaret and Ava. In either case, it represented a reaction on young Lyndon's part to the fire-and-brimstone preachers he encountered in Baptist circles and in local camp meetings. He gravitated instead to the more liberal and tolerant Disciples group, with their emphasis on good works.[3]

---

2. Quoted in Randall B. Woods, *LBJ: Architect of American Ambition* (New York: Free Press, 2006), 38. Regarding Lyndon Johnson's character, see Bill Moyers, *Moyers on America* (New York: New Press, 2004), 159–80. Moyers describes Johnson as "thirteen of the most interesting and difficult men I've ever met" (Moyers, *Moyers on America*, 159).

3. Woods, *LBJ*, 41.

Lyndon's baptism was also, almost certainly, a manifestation of adolescent rebellion. "I marched right home and told Momma," he later recalled. Rebekah wept. "She said that all of us were Baptists," Lyndon said, "and I was the only one that joined the Christian Church."[4]

Johnson himself, however, evinced little piety, and what little he showed during his long career of public life could properly be called perfunctory, even performative.

Lyndon Johnson invoked the deity on the evening of John F. Kennedy's assassination, November 22, 1963. After taking the oath of office aboard *Air Force One* at Love Field in Dallas and flying back to Washington with the casket of the slain president and with his widow, the new president faced a bank of microphones. "We have suffered a loss that cannot be weighed," he said. "I will do my best. That is all I can do. I ask for your help—and God's."[5]

Four days later, in his first appearance before Congress as president, Johnson memorably called on Americans to "put an end to the teaching and the preaching of hate and evil and violence. Let us turn away from the fanatics of the far left and the far right, from the apostles of bitterness and bigotry, from those defiant of law, and those who pour venom into our Nation's bloodstream." Johnson spoke about the "evil moment" in Dallas that had brought the nation together, and he called on Congress to pass civil-rights legislation: "no memorial oration or eulogy could more eloquently honor

---

4. Quoted in Woods, *LBJ,* 41.

5. Quoted in Merle Miller, *Lyndon: An Oral Biography* (New York: G. P. Putnam's Sons, 1980), 322.

President Kennedy's memory than the earliest possible passage of the civil rights bill for which he fought so long. We have talked long enough in this country about equal rights. We have talked for one hundred years or more. It is time now to write the next chapter, and to write it in the books of law."[6]

Johnson's stubborn engagement in Vietnam has tended to obfuscate his domestic achievements, notably the passage of the Civil Rights Act of 1964 and the Voting Rights Act of 1965. Both of these initiatives were significant, especially coming from a son of the South. But they also, together with his Great Society programs to end poverty and to provide health care for the elderly, derived from his understanding of the faith. Johnson could hardly be accused of theological sophistication, but he had gleaned from his parents at least the rudiments of a kind of "golden rule" Christianity.

Johnson's father had been a state legislator in Texas who opposed the Ku Klux Klan. As Sam Houston Johnson had said of Sam Ealy Johnson, he believed "in the dignity of all human beings regardless of race or creed." Rebekah Johnson imbued the first of her five children with a slightly different, albeit complementary, conviction. "At the center of my mother's philosophy," Johnson recalled, "was the belief that the strong must care for the weak. From the early days when she knew that I was to be the strongest of the five—with the most ambition and self-discipline and the most successful—she made me feel responsible for the weaker ones in the family."[7]

---

6. *Public Papers of the Presidents of the United States: Lyndon B. Johnson, 1963–64* (Washington, DC: Government Printing Office, 1965), 8–10.

7. Quoted in Woods, *LBJ*, 38; quoted in Doris Kearns Goodwin, *Lyndon Johnson and the American Dream* (New York: St. Martin's, 1976), 55.

Those principles informed Johnson's domestic initiatives, and his concern for those less advantaged was most apparent in his push for civil rights, even though he understood the political costs. Johnson had not been an advocate for integration throughout most of his career, although, as Senate majority leader, he did push the Civil Rights Act of 1957 through Congress. Being thrust into the presidency afforded him an opportunity to atone for his earlier neglect of the issue. "Most of us don't have a second chance to correct the mistakes of our youth," Johnson told a reporter who asked about his sudden interest in civil rights as president. "I do and I am." Johnson pushed for racial equality, despite the political ramifications. Late at night on July 2, 1964, after Johnson had signed the landmark Civil Rights Act earlier that day, Bill Moyers found the president in an uncharacteristically melancholy mood. "I think we just delivered the South to the Republican party for a long time to come," he said.[8]

Tragically, Johnson applied this same stronger-looking-after-the-weaker rationale to Vietnam. "There is," he told the nation in 1966, "a great responsibility on the strong. The oldest member of the family has got to look after the smaller ones and protect them when the wolf comes to the door." Johnson used this credo to justify his continued prosecution of the war, an extension of his understanding of the golden rule. As president, Lyndon Johnson had the biblical injunction, "Do unto others as you would have others do unto you," emblazoned on his stock of presidential gifts, along side of the presidential seal and the initials LBJ.[9]

More substantively, Johnson believed, as he told a group of civil-rights leaders in 1964, that "social problems are moral problems

8. Moyers, *Moyers on America,* 165, 167.

9. Quoted in Goodwin, *Lyndon Johnson,* 56, x.

on a large scale." Any religion, Johnson continued, "which did not struggle to remove oppression from the world of men would not be able to create the world of spirit," and it fell to the church to "be the first to awake to individual suffering" and "reawaken the conscience" of the United States.[10]

Johnson had already been assured of the support of the National Council of Churches in his efforts to end segregation. "We did not, of course, need any reassurances regarding your deep commitment to the cause of racial justice in America, for you have made your position crystal clear on numerous occasions by word and deed," the high-ranking executive of the council wrote to the president after their meeting on December 9, 1963. "But we did want you to know our full commitment to the civil rights struggle and of our desire to assist your administration in any way we can to help bring about the speediest passage of the Civil Rights Bill."[11]

Johnson's "Great Society" meant to build on the reawakening of conscience that, he believed, had been set in motion by John Kennedy. On a sunny afternoon, May 22, 1964, Johnson addressed a crowd of eighty thousand gathered for commencement exercises at the University of Michigan football stadium in Ann Arbor. Amid a society of plenty, Johnson said, "The challenge of the next half-century is whether we have the wisdom to use that wealth to enrich and elevate our national life, and to advance the quality of our American civilization." He summoned his audience to rise to the challenge of constructing a Great Society. "There

---

10. Quoted in Woods, *LBJ*, 465.

11. Letter, Robert W. Spike (executive director, Commission on Religion and Race, National Council of the Churches of Christ) to Lyndon B. Johnson, December 13, 1963, Name Files [National Council of the Churches of Christ], White House Central Files, Lyndon B. Johnson Library.

are those timid souls who say this battle cannot be won," he concluded, "that we are condemned to a soulless wealth. I do not agree. We have the power to shape the civilization that we want. But we need your will, your labor, your hearts, if we are to build that kind of society."[12]

Before Johnson could build the Great Society, however, he had to stand for election as president in his own right. Although Johnson faced no opposition for the Democratic nomination—he was nominated by acclamation—the Republicans countered with Barry Goldwater, United States senator from Arizona, a strong conservative who enjoyed the support of many theologically conservative Protestants, including (apparently) Billy Graham. The Johnson Presidential Library in Austin, Texas, contains a secondhand account of a visit by Goldwater's representatives to Graham's home in Montreat, North Carolina, in advance of the Republican National Convention. According to the memorandum, the Goldwater delegation wanted to sound out the evangelist about the possibility that he would become Goldwater's running mate. "Surprisingly enough, Graham was greatly pleased, flattered and impressed," the document reads. "The matter was discussed for several hours." Graham finally demurred, giving as his reason the fact that there was not sufficient time for him to make a transition from preacher to politician in the eyes of the public.[13]

---

12. Quoted in Woods, *LBJ*, 466.

13. Memorandum, Earle B. Mayfield Jr. (attorney, Dallas, Texas) to Lyndon B. Johnson, July 21, 1966, Papers of Lyndon Baines Johnson, Box 227a, Lyndon B. Johnson Library. I emphasize that this is a secondhand narrative; I have not been able to verify the authenticity of the meeting between Graham and the Goldwater delegation, though it is clear that, at the very least, many members of Graham's own family were partial to Goldwater.

Graham was besieged by telegrams—some sixty thousand in a single day, according to one account—calling on the evangelist to endorse Goldwater. Graham's father-in-law, L. Nelson Bell, was a fervent partisan for Goldwater, and Graham's daughter, Anne, publicly endorsed the Republican. Johnson took Graham's wavering seriously enough to admonish him, "Now, Billy, you stay out of politics." And the president took the additional precaution of inviting Graham and his wife to stay at the White House during the final weekend of the campaign, presumably to thwart any last-minute gesture or comment that might be interpreted as support for Johnson's Republican opponent.[14]

Johnson's landslide victory—forty-four states and 61 percent of the popular vote—in the presidential election of 1964, abetted by the lingering grief over Kennedy's assassination, provided Johnson with the mandate he sought to inaugurate the Great Society. "Congratulations on your tremendous victory. There has never been anything like it in the history of America!" Graham enthused. "I am sure that the responsibilities of such a mandate must be staggering," he added. "I shall do everything in my power to call upon Christians everywhere to pray for you daily that God's strength and wisdom will be yours."[15]

Following the election, Johnson moved rapidly to enact his vision of the Great Society, one that would banish poverty and racial discrimination and inadequate access to health care, especially for the elderly. But those reforms were steadily, and increas-

14. Marshall Frady, *Billy Graham: A Parable of American Righteousness* (Boston: Little, Brown, 1979), 266, 352; cf. Billy Graham, *Just As I Am: The Autobiography of Billy Graham* (San Francisco: HarperOne, 1997), 407.

15. Letter, Billy Graham to Lyndon B. Johnson, November 10, 1964, Papers of Lyndon Baines Johnson, Box 227a, Lyndon B. Johnson Library.

ingly, undermined by Johnson's persistent prosecution of the war in Vietnam. The costs of the war bled resources from his domestic programs, and the mounting popular opposition undermined the moral authority of his vision of the Great Society. Soon, religious voices began to weigh in on the war.

"Much as I deplore the spread of Communism in Asia, it seems to me that methods of sheer force are not only unavailing but also tend to be immoral and unjust, when they are used without wisdom in an attempt to check the Communists," Thomas Merton, the Trappist monk, wrote to the president early in 1965. "I therefore wish to suggest most strongly that something be done to change this situation, and I hope that peace can be negotiated by an international group where all those concerned can feel satisfied that they have had a just hearing. In short, I think the U.S. military would do more for democracy if they got out of Vietnam than they are doing now." Dorothy Day of the Catholic Worker movement also registered her opposition to the war, urging Johnson in a telegram to "TAKE STEPS TO CEASE HOSTILITIES IN SOUTH VIET NAM AND WITHDRAW US TROOPS AS SOON AS POSSIBLE."[16]

Philip Berrigan, another Roman Catholic, a priest who would emerge as one of the Vietnam War's most implacable opponents, sent a cable to the White House just a few days after Merton's letter:

AS YOU HAVE IGNORED APPEALS FROM POPE PAUL, U THANT,

PRESIDENT DE GAULLE AND SO MANY OTHERS WE HAVE

16. Letter, Thomas Merton to Lyndon B. Johnson, February 20, 1965, Name Files, White House Central Files, Lyndon B. Johnson Library; Telegram, Dorothy Day and Thomas Cornell to Lyndon B. Johnson, 11/12/1964, Name Files, White House Central Files, Lyndon B. Johnson Library.

LITTLE HOPE OUR PROTEST WILL CHALLENGE YOUR WILL
TO CONTINUE AND EVEN WIDEN THE WAR IN VIETNAM
BUT WE ARE SADDENED AND ANGERED TO SEE OUR NA-
TION ENTER THE MIRE OF OBLIVION SO IGNOBLY. WE
MUST AGAIN AS BLOOD IS STILL WET ON THE GROUND IN
VIETNAM. ASK YOU TO CALL CEASE FIRE FOLLOWED BY NE-
GOTIATION AND THE WITHDRAWAL OF AMERICAN TROOPS
AND MILITARY SUPPORT

Other Catholic voices raised more specific concerns about the conduct of the war itself, specifically the practice of "bombing targets in or very near to population centers in North Vietnam." The head of Catholic Charities for the Diocese of Indianapolis weighed in with his view: "I do not think wars of violence are in accord with the teaching of Christ and I do not think they bring about the goals we seek through them."[17]

Protestants also began to raise objections. On February 25, 1965, just weeks into Johnson's elected term in office, the general board of the National Council of Churches, meeting in Portland, Oregon, called on the administration to "engage in persistent efforts to negotiate a cease fire and a settlement of the war which will attempt to achieve the independence, freedom and self-determination of the people of South Vietnam."

---

17. Telegram, Philip Berrigan, et al. to Lyndon B. Johnson, March 2, 1965, Name Files, White House Central Files, Lyndon B. Johnson Library; Press release from Catholic Association for International Peace, March 22, 1968, Name Files [United States Catholic Conference], White House Central Files, Lyndon B. Johnson Library; Letter, Donald Schmidlin (director, Catholic Charities, Archdiocese of Indianapolis) to Lyndon B. Johnson, December 22, 1966, Name Files [Catholic, C], White House Central Files, Lyndon B. Johnson Library.

Later that same year, the president of the National Council of Churches voiced his fears that Johnson was backing away from a negotiated settlement in Vietnam. "This, it seems to us, would be a self-defeating move denying the basic purposes in Viet-Nam, and would be a tragic backing away from the course you have so courageously evolved," he wrote. "We trust that you will continue to use every possible diplomatic channel and especially the potentialities within the United Nations system to press for honorable negotiations."[18]

Many conservative Protestants, on the other hand, persisted in seeing the Vietnam conflict through the lens of the Cold War. "The Communists are moving fast toward their goal of world revolution," Graham wrote to the president in 1965, adding that Johnson "could be the man that helped save Christian civilization." "Assure the president that the National and World Council of Churches do not speak for many people," Edward K. Rogers of the Lutheran Church in America wrote from West Virginia. "They do not speak for the great throng of us who opposed and fought Hitler and Mussolini, and who oppose a similar threat from communism today." Harold Lindsell, editor of *Christianity Today* magazine, weighed in to support Johnson's policies in Southeast Asia. "America wants peace and is forced to use war to secure it," his editorial in the March 4, 1966, issue declared. "Had there

---

18. "Resolution on Vietnam," General Board of the National Council of Churches (meeting in Portland, Oregon), February 25, 1965, Name Files [National Council of the Churches of Christ], White House Central Files, Lyndon B. Johnson Library; Letter, Reuben H. Mueller (president, National Council of the Churches of Christ) to Lyndon B. Johnson, September 24, 1965, Name Files [National Council of the Churches of Christ], White House Central Files, Lyndon B. Johnson Library.

been no Communist aggression in Viet Nam, America would not be involved in the present conflict."[19]

Another evangelical, however, who registered early dissent against the war in Vietnam was Mark O. Hatfield, the Republican governor of Oregon who won election to the Senate in 1966. In his keynote address to the Republican National Convention in 1964, Hatfield had sounded the alarm about Vietnam. Speaking of the Johnson administration, Hatfield asked, "Why, why do they fear telling the American people what our foreign policy is?" He added: "Even when American boys are dying in a war without a name." The next year, at a meeting of the nation's governors, Hatfield registered the lone dissent to a resolution supporting Johnson's conduct of the war.[20]

Hatfield stood his ground, even in the face of what Washington insiders called "the Johnson treatment," a fiercely intensive personal lobbying effort by the president, a technique he had honed to perfection as majority leader in the Senate. But when Johnson made moves late in 1965 to seek a negotiated conclusion to the war, Hatfield cabled the president with his encour-

19. Letter, Billy Graham to Lyndon B. Johnson, July 11, 1965, President's Appointment File Diary Backup, July 17, 1965, Box 19, Lyndon B. Johnson Library; Letter, Edward K. Rogers (assistant to the president for stewardship and evangelism, Western Pennsylvania—West Virginia Synod, Lutheran Church in America) to Bill Moyers, February 27, 1966, Name Files [National Council of the Churches of Christ], White House Central Files, Lyndon B. Johnson Library; Route slip, Paul M. Popple to Benjamin H. Read, April 29, 1965, Name Files [Christianity Today], White House Central Files, Lyndon B. Johnson Library; "W.C.C. and Viet Nam," Christianity Today, March 4, 1966, 31.

20. Mark O. Hatfield, with Diane N. Solomon, Against the Grain: Reflections of a Rebel Republican (Ashland, OR: White Cloud Press, 2001), 95. Hatfield was also the lone dissenter to a similar resolution at the governor's conference the following year (Hatfield and Solomon, Against the Grain, 102).

agement and support. By 1967, however, with little progress toward American withdrawal from Vietnam, a good deal of religious sentiment turned against the war. "We are certain that the great majority of people in our churches urgently desire a prompt cease-fire followed by an early and honorable negotiated peace in Viet Nam," representatives of the National Council of Churches wrote on April 10, 1967, "and that they will support every effort on your part to secure these ends without further intensification of military measures."[21]

At nine o'clock on March 31, 1968, Lyndon Johnson sat at his desk in the Oval Office to address the American public yet again about the war in Vietnam. "We are prepared to move immediately toward peace through negotiations," he said, announcing his decision unilaterally to de-escalate the war. "One day, my fellow citizens, there will be peace in Southeast Asia," he promised. Then, drawing a deep breath, Johnson continued: "Fifty-two months and 10 days ago, in a moment of tragedy and trauma, the duties of this office fell upon me. I asked then for your help and God's, that we might continue America on its course, binding up our wounds, healing our history, moving forward in new unity, to clear the American agenda and to keep the American commitment for all of our people." Then the bombshell. "With America's sons in the fields far away, with America's future under challenge right

21. Telegram, Mark O. Hatfield to Lyndon B. Johnson, December 31, 1965, Name Files [Hatfield, Mark O.], White House Central Files, Lyndon B. Johnson Library; Letter, Arthur S. Flemming (president, National Council of the Churches of Christ) and R. H. Edwin Espy (general secretary, National Council of the Churches of Christ) to Lyndon B. Johnson, April 10, 1967, Name Files [National Council of the Churches of Christ], White House Central Files, Lyndon B. Johnson Library. On Johnson's efforts to influence Hatfield, see Hatfield and Solomon, *Against the Grain,* 99–100.

here at home, with our hopes and the world's hopes for peace in the balance every day, I do not believe that I should devote an hour or a day of my time to any personal partisan causes or to any duties other than the awesome duties of this office—the Presidency of your country." Johnson concluded in his deliberate speaking style: "Accordingly, I shall not seek, and I will not accept, the nomination of my party for another term as your President."[22]

Several weeks earlier Eugene McCarthy, United States senator from Minnesota, had embarrassed Johnson in New Hampshire by drawing 42 percent of the votes in that state's Democratic primary. Robert F. Kennedy, brother of the slain president and now United States senator from New York, entered the Democratic primaries shortly thereafter. Rather than mount an uncertain run for renomination, Johnson withdrew. Several days later Graham sent Johnson a telegram expressing the wish "THAT GOD MAY GRANT YOU PEACE OF SOUL COURAGE OF HEART AND WISDOM OF MIND."[23]

Although Graham had forged a cordial relationship with Johnson, and the two of them frequently exchanged encomiums, the evangelist could hardly have been disappointed by Johnson's decision not to stand for reelection. The absence of an incumbent coupled with the ensuing chaos in the Democratic Party—which was compounded by the assassinations of Martin Luther King Jr.

---

22. *Public Papers of the Presidents of the United States: Lyndon B. Johnson, 1968–69* (Washington, DC: Government Printing Office, 1970), 469–76.

23. Telegram, Billy Graham to Lyndon B. Johnson, April 6, 1968, Papers of Lyndon Baines Johnson, Box 227a, Lyndon B. Johnson Library. Graham contends that Johnson had confided in him of his decision not to run for reelection months earlier; Graham, *Just As I Am,* 414.

and Robert Kennedy—provided a huge opening for Richard Nixon, who claimed the Republican nomination at his party's national convention in August. Johnson's vice president, Hubert Humphrey, eventually won the Democratic nomination after a bruising struggle, literally and figuratively, in Chicago.

Graham had met Richard Nixon's mother, Hannah, a Quaker, after his 1949 evangelistic crusade in Los Angeles. She informed the young evangelist that her late husband had taken their three sons to hear another evangelist, Paul Rader, and that all three boys had responded to the preacher's invitation to be converted to evangelical Christianity. Richard Nixon played the piano for Sunday school and sang in the choir at the Friends Church in East Whittier. Graham met Nixon himself in the Senate dining room a year or two after Graham had met Nixon's mother. Both men had gained notoriety because they were anti-communist crusaders, and they immediately struck up a friendship that would extend until Nixon's death in 1994. Throughout the decades, and despite Nixon's persistent and demonstrated pattern of venality, Graham clung to the belief that Nixon was a man of deep and abiding faith, and, in Graham's words, "this godly heritage did as much as anything to make us compatible."[24]

Although Graham frequently protested that his advice to politicians was invariably spiritual and not political, that has not always rung true. Beginning with Dwight Eisenhower, Graham volunteered to undertake diplomatic missions in the course of his travels. He encouraged Nixon to choose an evangelical member

---

24. Richard Nixon, *RN: The Memoirs of Richard Nixon* (New York: Grosset & Dunlap, 1978), 288. Graham's understanding of Nixon's conversion appears in *Just As I Am,* 440–41.

of Congress and a former missionary to China, Walter Judd, as his running mate in 1960. During the 1968 Republican National Convention, Graham pressed for the selection of Mark Hatfield, the evangelical opponent of the Vietnam War now serving in the Senate. Hatfield in fact emerged as one of Nixon's two finalists for the vice-presidential nomination. Nixon dithered until the last minute before finally selecting Spiro Agnew, governor of Maryland, as part of Nixon's "southern strategy" to siphon Democratic votes in the South.

Once in office, Nixon instituted worship services in the White House. Unsurprisingly, Graham conducted the initial service just six days after having offered a prayer at Nixon's inauguration, in the course of which he had thanked the Almighty that "thou hast permitted Richard Nixon to lead us at this momentous hour of history." The format of the first White House gathering replicated the pattern of Graham's revival crusades: congregational singing led by Cliff Barrows, vocal solos by George Beverly Shea, and preaching by Graham himself. Graham conducted four of those services throughout the course of Nixon's tenure in the White House; Norman Vincent Peale also preached four times, and others were led by an array of Protestant, Roman Catholic, and Jewish leaders.[25]

The worship services in the White House, however, quickly devolved into political theater. Early on, Charles W. Colson, Nixon's assistant, received an "action memo" urging him to act quickly on the "President's request that you develop a list of rich

---

25. Quoted in William Martin, *A Prophet with Honor: The Billy Graham Story* (New York: William Morrow & Co., 1991), 355; Graham, *Just As I Am*, 451.

people with strong religious interest to be invited to the White House church services."[26]

Whatever religious or spiritual benefit Nixon derived from these occasions was not immediately apparent in his conduct as president, although Graham himself detected vast reservoirs of piety and moral vision in the thirty-seventh president. "You have given moral and spiritual leadership to the nation at a time when we desperately needed it," Graham declared in a handwritten note near the end of Nixon's second year in office. "Thank you!"[27]

Others—many others—have tried to plumb the darkness of Nixon's psyche—the insecurity, the isolation, and the persistent paranoia that seemed to lurk behind every action, every decision. His predilection for furtive machinations, abetted by his equally paranoid associates, reached its apotheosis during the 1972 re-election campaign against Senator George S. McGovern of South Dakota, the Democratic nominee. Although Nixon's "dirty tricks" campaign operatives doubtless played a role in sabotaging the candidacies of other Democrats whom Nixon and his operatives regarded as more formidable opponents, thereby helping throw the nomination to McGovern, the senator's antiwar candidacy drew on the deep misgivings many Americans harbored about the war in Vietnam.

Despite a commanding lead in the polls and an overwhelming advantage in fund-raising, Nixon's campaign, the Committee to Re-Elect the President (known universally as CREEP),

---

26. Quoted in Martin, *Prophet with Honor*, 356.

27. Quoted in Martin, *Prophet with Honor*, 371.

dispatched burglars to the headquarters of the Democratic National Committee at the Watergate office complex in Washington. On the evening of June 17, 1972, Frank Wills, a security guard, noticed an unlocked door and, at 1:47 a.m., summoned the police. The ensuing arrest of the Watergate burglars precipitated a domino effect that would eventually topple Nixon's presidency. Several days after the break-in, on June 23, Nixon and his chief of staff, H. R. Haldeman, conspired in the Oval Office to cover up the incident and to impede efforts by the Federal Bureau of Investigation to investigate the matter.

Prodded in part by the intrepid efforts of two reporters from the *Washington Post,* Carl Bernstein and Bob Woodward, others began to take interest in what the White House repeatedly dismissed as a "third-rate burglary." Gradually, however, the magnitude of the Watergate scandal became apparent. Special prosecutors, fighting through the Nixon administration's persistent and determined efforts to subvert justice, finally began to secure convictions or plea bargains from White House officials.

Many of the Watergate felons "got religion" in the course of their sojourns through the criminal-justice system. Jeb Stuart Magruder, deputy director of Nixon's reelection campaign, for instance, attended Princeton Theological Seminary after his release from prison and became a Presbyterian minister. Charles Colson, widely known as Nixon's "hatchet man" who famously declared that he would run over his own grandmother to secure Nixon's reelection, converted to evangelical Christianity prior to entering a guilty plea in 1974 for obstruction of justice. Colson, who once had proposed firebombing the Brookings Institution, a Washington think tank with liberal leanings, founded an organization called Prison Fellowship and later functioned as a kind of elder statesman for the Religious Right.[28]

After a select committee of the United States Senate discovered that Nixon had installed an elaborate, secret taping system to record White House conversations, a legal battle ensued over the disposition of the tapes. The Supreme Court's unanimous ruling on July 24, 1974, that Nixon had to surrender the tapes, accelerated his downfall and forced his resignation less than three weeks later—after the House Judiciary Committee had approved three articles of impeachment. In the meantime, transcripts of the tapes were eventually released, detailing the extent of Nixon's duplicity and his repeated attempts to obstruct justice. On reading the transcripts, Graham, who had earlier characterized the Watergate scandal as "another sign of permissiveness" and who had assured Nixon of his "complete confidence in your personal integrity," declared that he was physically sickened—but not by Nixon's extra-legal maneuvers or by his attempts to subvert the Constitution. He was upset by his friend's use of foul language.[29] Hah

In his remarks at the Presidential Prayer Breakfast on January 30, 1969, just ten days after his first inauguration as president, Nixon had noted that his friend Billy Graham conducted a study of United States presidents and concluded that, although not all of them entered the White House with a strong faith, "all had left

---

28. Colson's autobiography, *Born Again,* published in 1976, became a best seller and, together with Jimmy Carter's meteoric rise to the presidency that same year, contributed to *Newsweek*'s designation of 1976 as "The Year of the Evangelical." Colson repented of his sins, but never of his archconservative politics.

29. Quoted in Martin, *Prophet with Honor,* 426, 427, 431; Graham, *Just As I Am,* 457.

the Presidency with a very deep religious faith." Whether Nixon himself fit that pattern is a question that has divided biographers. Graham himself remained lost in admiration for Nixon, referring to his friend as late as 1992 as one of the "great men" he had ever known.[30]

By the time Richard Nixon stabbed his fingers into the air at the door of the helicopter on August 9, 1974, in a final gesture of defiance, Americans had become well accustomed to a preacher named Billy at the White House. Billy Graham had been a fixture in the Nixon years, conducting worship services and offering private counsel to the beleaguered president. The ascension of Gerald R. Ford to the presidency introduced Americans to another preacher named Billy—Billy Zeoli.

Gerald Ford, formerly a member of Congress from Michigan, is the only president in American history never to have been elected either president or vice president. Under the provisions of the Twenty-fifth Amendment to the United States Constitution, which was passed by Congress in 1965 and ratified two years later, should a vacancy occur in the vice presidency, the president had the power to appoint a replacement, subject to a majority vote in both houses of Congress. Nixon appointed Ford as vice president following Spiro T. Agnew's resignation in October 1973, after he pleaded no contest to charges of corruption; Ford took the oath

---

30. "Remarks at the 17th Annual Presidential Prayer Breakfast," January 30, 1969. *Public Papers of Richard Nixon.* Richard M. Nixon Library and Birthplace; *Crusade: The Life of Billy Graham,* PBS documentary, prod. Randall Balmer (Chicago: WTTW, 1993).

of office on December 6, 1973. At three minutes after noon on August 9, 1974, Ford took another oath, this time as president. "Our long national nightmare is over," Ford declared. "Our Constitution works; our great Republic is a government of laws and not of men."

Ford, who was born Leslie Lynch King Jr. in Omaha, Nebraska, took the name of his adoptive father after his mother moved to Grand Rapids, Michigan, and remarried. He was reared an Episcopalian, an affiliation he retained throughout his life; during his time in the White House, his son Michael was a divinity student at Gordon-Conwell Theological Seminary.

Ford met Billy Zeoli, head of an evangelical organization called Gospel Films, based in Grand Rapids, when Ford was a member of Congress. Zeoli, a cartoonish figure with close ties to the archconservative DeVos family of Amway fame, had stopped by Ford's office to give him a Bible. The two struck up a conversation and a friendship that endured even beyond Ford's brief tenure in the White House. Every Monday morning of Ford's presidency, Zeoli's typewritten note would be placed on Ford's desk, with the heading "God's Got a Better Idea," a clever take-off on the Ford Motor Company's advertising campaign at the time: Ford's Got a Better Idea. Addressed "To Jerry From 'Z,'" a typical missive would read like this:

God's Got A Better Idea
Week of August 18, 1975
To Jerry
From "Z"

VERSE

Matthew 8:25

Living Bible

#75 "And His disciples came to Him and awake Him, saying, 'Lord, save us: we perish!'"

PRAYER

Dear God,

How many times have I shouted to you, "Lord, save me I'm sinking."

You always respond and help me—

sometimes not as quickly as my impatience demands,

and other times not in the exact way I want You to.

It is hard for me to understand why You are not fed up with me.

It is hard for me to understand why I don't learn more quickly—

that if I would follow the principles for living that You lay down,

I would be in danger of sinking less often.

Lord, I will try to apply what You have taught me.

Thanks for being there when I have to shout, "Lord, save me from sinking!"

In Jesus' Name,

AMEN

Copyright © 1974

William J. Zeoli

All Rights Reserved

Zeoli sent 146 such devotionals to the White House in the course of Ford's presidency.[31]

Zeoli also sent letters and telegrams to Ford's senior staff members offering political advice, requesting appointments with Vice President Nelson Rockefeller or Secretary of State Henry Kissinger, or demanding that a car be sent to pick him up at a Washington hotel. Zeoli signed his missives "In His love and mine." By the fall of 1974, just weeks into Ford's presidency, the *St. Louis Post-Dispatch* published an article quoting Zeoli as saying that he had noticed "a definite Christian growth" in Ford over the previous nine months. Zeoli also said that he had been with Ford just prior to his first press conference as president: "The door was shut, there were no phone calls, no interruptions—just me, the President and God."[32]

The press began to pick up on Ford's relationship to this somewhat odd and self-promoting impresario from Grand Rapids. Some observers noted that Graham had not visited the White

---

31. Memo, Billy Zeoli to Gerald R. Ford, August 18, 1975, "Religious Matters 3/1/75—1/20/77" folder, White House Central Files Subject File, Box 1, Gerald R. Ford Library; Nancy Gibbs and Michael Duffy, "The Other Born-again President," *Time,* January 15, 2007, 40. The Zeoli memo is used by permission.

32. Eric L. Zoeckler, "Ford Had Sought Will of God, Minister Says," *St. Louis Post-Dispatch*, September 12, 1974, 5C. Regarding Zeoli's communications with White House staff, see, for instance, Letter, Billy Zeoli to Ron Nessen, January 16, 1975, Name Files, [Zeoli, Billy (1)], White House Central Files, Box 3539, Gerald R. Ford Papers, Gerald R. Ford Library; Letter, Billy Zeoli to Warren Rustand, February 13, 1975, Name Files, [Zeoli, Billy (1)], White House Central Files, Box 3539, Gerald R. Ford Papers, Gerald R. Ford Library; Telegram, Billy Zeoli to Warren Rustand, September 19, 1975, Name Files, [Zeoli, Billy (1)], White House Central Files, Box 3539, Gerald R. Ford Papers, Gerald R. Ford Library.

House, whereas Zeoli was a regular. Soon the White House, even the president himself, started to retreat. When an internal memo warned that the *Chicago Tribune* planned to do an article on Zeoli, who had described himself to the reporter as "the President's spiritual adviser who prays with the President in the Oval Office," Ford struck out "spiritual adviser" and wrote: "A very good friend of the family. I do, when he visits, pray with him."[33]

Graham may not have been a visible presence at 1600 Pennsylvania Avenue, but he was working behind the scenes to secure a pardon for Nixon. Graham, fearing for Nixon's life if he had to face the ordeal of a humiliating trial and possibly a prison sentence, communicated his sentiments to the White House, including Alexander Haig, Ford's chief of staff. Haig agreed with Graham and asked him to expect a phone call from Ford to discuss the matter. After Graham had made his case, Ford acknowledged that it was a "tough call" and concluded by assuring Graham that "I'm giving it a lot of thought and prayer."[34]

On Sunday morning, September 8, a week later, Ford went to St. John's Episcopal Church, across Lafayette Park from the White House, and then prepared a speech announcing his decision to pardon his predecessor. The television camera went live at 11:05 a.m. "The Constitution is the supreme law of our land

---

33. Memo, Jack Hushen to Bob Hartmann, September 27, 1974, Name Files, [Zeoli, Billy], Robert T. Hartmann Files, Gerald R. Ford Library. On the visits of Zeoli and the absence of Graham, see Lester Kinsolving, "A New Preacher Comes to the White House," *Houston Post,* January 4, 1975.

34. Quoted in Graham, *Just As I Am,* 468; cf. Gibbs and Duffy, "Other Born-again President," 41. There seems to be some confusion between the Gibbs-Duffy account and Graham's recollection regarding whether Ford's call to Graham occurred on a Saturday or a Sunday.

and it governs our actions as citizens," Ford began. "Only the laws of God, which govern our consciences, are superior to it." He acknowledged the "American tragedy in which we all have played a part" and that "serious allegations and accusations hang like a sword over our former president's head, threatening his health." Ford, speaking to the nation, declared that "my first consideration is to be true to my own convictions and my own conscience" and that his conscience demanded a pardon. "I do believe, with all my heart and mind and spirit, that I, not as President but as a humble servant of God, will receive justice without mercy if I fail to show mercy," he said. Then he read from the proclamation: "Now, therefore, I, Gerald R. Ford, President of the United States, pursuant to the pardon power conferred upon me by Article II, Section 2, of the Constitution, have granted and by these presents do grant a full, free, and absolute pardon unto Richard Nixon for all offenses against the United States which he, Richard Nixon, has committed or may have committed or taken part in during the period from July [January] 20, 1969 through August 9, 1974."[35]

Reaction was swift and not especially favorable, even within the White House. Although Ford had retained many of the staff members and cabinet secretaries from the Nixon administration, one of his first and most obvious moves as president was to replace Ron Ziegler, Nixon's press secretary, with someone of sterling integrity. Ford chose Jerald F. ter Horst, a highly respected reporter for the *Grand Rapids Press* and, beginning in 1953, a reporter, Washington bureau chief, and eventually a columnist for the *Detroit News*.

---

35. John Woolley and Gerhard Peters, The American Presidency Project [online]. Santa Barbara, CA: University of California (hosted), Gerhard Peters (database): http://www.presidency.ucsb.edu/ws/?pid=4695.

Ford had known ter Horst for years; the president respected both his journalistic skills and, more important, his integrity. Because Ziegler had become so entangled and complicit in Nixon's prevarications, Ford needed to appoint someone who would bring credibility to the White House. Jerald ter Horst was his first appointment, a choice that met with almost universal approbation.

Not even a month into the job, however, ter Horst faced a moral crisis. When he had learned that Saturday of the president's decision preemptively to pardon his predecessor, ter Horst stayed up most of the night struggling with his conscience. He determined that he could not defend Ford's action, so he penned a three-paragraph letter of resignation. "I cannot find words to adequately express my respect and admiration for you over the many years of our friendship and my belief that you could heal the wounds and unite our country in this most critical time in our nation's history," ter Horst began. "So it is with much regret, after long soul-searching, that I must inform you that I cannot in good conscience support your decision to pardon former President Nixon even before he has been charged with the commission of any crime." Ter Horst noted the absence of any parallel pardon for those who had evaded the draft during the war in Vietnam, and he suggested that many of Nixon's surrogates—those who had carried out his orders or were acting on his behalf—faced similar troubles to those Ford had cited to justify Nixon's pardon. "Thus it is with a heavy heart that I hereby tender my resignation as Press Secretary to the President, effective today," ter Horst concluded. "My prayers nonetheless remain with you, sir."[36]

---

36. Letter (typewritten), Jerald F. ter Horst to Gerald R. Ford, September 8, 1974, filed "Ter Horst Resignation as Press Secretary," James E. Connor Files, 1974–77, Box 19, Gerald R. Ford Library.

When Ford received ter Horst's letter of resignation, he dispatched a top aide to talk him out of resigning, but ter Horst was resolute. He sent a second, handwritten note: "Regretfully, I find I must hold to my original resignation decision effective today. . . . God Bless you, sir—again, I'm sorry it is necessary for me to resign." The follow-up note bore the time 11:15, the same moment that Ford was announcing his decision to the nation.[37]

Gerald Ford's preemptive pardon of Richard Nixon was meant to salve the wounds of a nation and to put Watergate to rest. While weighing his decision, Ford had dispatched his White House counsel to Leon Jaworski, the special prosecutor for Watergate, to learn how long Jaworski expected Nixon's trial to last. When the word returned that Jaworski expected the trial to extend at least two years, Ford concluded that he must act to spare the nation that long ordeal of recrimination, division, and uncertainty.[38]

Newspaper editorial pages criticized the decision, and many Democratic leaders reviled Ford for the pardon. Senator Walter F. Mondale of Minnesota introduced a constitutional amendment that would provide for a two-thirds vote in both houses of Congress to overturn future presidential pardons. "Mr. Ford's pardon of former President Nixon proves that the issue of presidential

37. Letter (handwritten), Jerald F. ter Horst to Gerald R. Ford, September 8, 1974, filed "Ter Horst Resignation as Press Secretary," James E. Connor Files, 1974–77, Box 19, Gerald R. Ford Library.

38. James Cannon, "Gerald R. Ford, 1974–1977," in Character Above All: Ten Presidents from FDR to George Bush, ed. Robert A. Wilson (New York: Simon & Schuster, 1995), 162.

accountability is still with us—and unresolved," Mondale noted. Edward M. Kennedy, Democrat of Massachusetts, remarked: "The tidal wave of national criticism over his pardon of Mr. Nixon should have shown the President that his instincts are clearly out of touch with the vast majority of the people of America."[39]

The obvious suspicion was that Ford had agreed to pardon Nixon before the latter relinquished his office. Nixon's chief of staff, Alexander Haig, had, in fact, approached Ford, then the vice president, to propose such an arrangement, but Ford refused. In an attempt to dispel the suspicion, Ford took the unprecedented step of appearing directly before the House Judiciary Committee. "There was no deal. Period," he declared bluntly. "Under no circumstances."[40]

Not all critics were appeased—not by any means. Some clergy lauded Ford's decision, including a Unitarian Universalist minister, Duncan E. Littlefair, in Ford's hometown of Grand Rapids. "I feel very remiss in not having written to express my appreciation for the tremendous sermon you gave on Sunday, September 15th, following my pardoning of former President Nixon," Ford wrote in appreciation. "Naturally, having known very well over the years how very vehemently you disagreed with the former President's policies, and that you seldom concurred with any of mine, the eloquent way in which you defended my action was

---

39. Press release, Office of Senator Walter F. Mondale, September 8, 1974; Press release, Office of Senator Edward M. Kennedy, September 10, 1974. It is worth noting that Kennedy came, in time, to see the wisdom of Ford's pardon—a sentiment that emerged in the aftermath of Ford's death in 2006.

40. Quoted in Cannon, "Gerald R. Ford," 164.

extremely moving." Graham, who had pushed for the pardon, remained silent.[41]

The presidential pardon of Nixon generated controversy and reopened old wounds, precisely what Ford had hoped to avoid. Ford's act of mercy, at least as it was understood by some, became the defining moment of his presidency. But it was interpreted by others as yet another cynical gesture, following directly as it did on what was—to that point, at least—the most corrupt and cynical presidency in American history. As Gerald Ford prepared to seek the presidency in his own right in 1976, he faced an electorate that had grown tired of Lyndon Johnson's deceptions in Vietnam, weary of Richard Nixon's endless prevarications, and ready, it seemed, once again to consider matters of faith and character in assessing their choice for president.

---

41. Letter, Gerald R. Ford to Duncan E. Littlefair, October 28, 1976, file "Nixon, Richard Milhous," Vertical File, Gerald R. Ford Library.

John Paul II and Jimmy Carter at the White House in 1979, during the pontiff's first visit to the United States. In the course of the 1976 campaign, Carter withstood intense pressure from Catholic bishops to pledge to outlaw abortion. He insisted that, although he was "personally opposed" to abortion, he would abide by the law of the land.

THREE

# BORN AGAIN

*Jimmy Carter, Redeemer President, and*
*the Rise of the Religious Right*

The meteoric ascent of Jimmy Carter from an obscure, one-term governor of Georgia to the presidency of the United States remains one of the most dramatic stories in the annals of American politics. Abetted by the political chicanery of Richard Nixon and his minions, by the dark depravity of Watergate and the ignominy of Vietnam, Carter burst onto the scene at precisely the moment when Americans were searching for a kind of savior, someone to lead them out of the wilderness of shame and corruption to the promised land of redemption and rehabilitation. His promise that he would "never knowingly lie" to the American people, and his declaration that the United States deserved a government "as good as the American people" struck a chord. Americans responded by electing Carter the thirty-ninth president of the United States on November 2, 1976.

The 1976 election was significant in that many of Carter's supporters were evangelical Christians, a large number of whom had not been politically active until then. Many had voted, albeit with little enthusiasm, but many others shunned politics altogether out of some combination of indifference and a conviction that the imminent return of Jesus in apocalyptic judgment rendered all attempts at social amelioration irrelevant. Since the conclusion of the Scopes trial in 1925, many evangelicals thought of themselves as culturally marginal. Carter's declaration that he was a "born again" Christian caught their attention. Southern evangelicals in particular responded favorably to the fact that this Southern Baptist Sunday school teacher was evidently a man of deep piety. They gave him their support—and their votes.

If Carter's political ascendancy represents one of the most dramatic stories in the history of American politics, the rapid turning against Carter by many of the very same evangelicals who had supported him in 1976 is one of the most striking paradoxes of American politics. The years of Carter's presidency saw the formation of conservative evangelicals into a formidable voting bloc, the Religious Right, which in turn mobilized to defeat him in 1980.

In the heat of the campaign for the North Carolina Democratic primary in 1976, Jimmy Carter's declaration that he was a "born again" Christian received intense media scrutiny. "Incidentally, we've checked this out," one network anchor solemnly informed his audience. "Being 'born again' is not a bizarre experience of the voice of God from the mountaintop. It's a fairly common experience known to millions of Americans—especially if you're Baptist."[1]

---

1. Quoted in Wesley G. Pippert, comp., *The Spiritual Journey of Jimmy Carter: In His Own Words* (New York: Macmillan, 1978), 2.

Millions of American evangelicals, Baptist and otherwise, needed no such explanation. The term "born again" appears in the King James Version of John 3 in the New Testament. Nicodemus, a Jewish leader, visited Jesus by night to ask how he could be admitted into the kingdom of heaven; Jesus replied that he must be "born again." Evangelical Christians generally interpret this to mean that a conversion, or "born again" experience, spells the difference between salvation and damnation. Billy Graham, for instance, invites his auditors to "make a decision for Christ," by which he means that they should "accept Jesus into their hearts" and thereby be "saved." All of these are roughly synonymous terms, but they point to the centrality of religious conversion in the lives of evangelicals. Indeed, this emphasis on conversion, coupled with the conviction that the Bible is God's revelation to humanity and therefore should be taken very seriously, comprise the very definition of what it means to be an evangelical Christian.[2]

Jimmy Carter's conversion came early in life. Reared in a Southern Baptist household in Plains, Georgia, he memorized his first Bible verse at age four: "God is love." He accepted Jesus as his savior—became "born again"—at eleven and was baptized. The sequence here is crucial. Unlike Roman Catholics or Episcopalians or Methodists or many other Christian denominations, Baptists believe that the rite (not sacrament) of baptism should be full immersion (not sprinkling) and should be done as

2. For a more extended discussion of the definition and the phenomenon of evangelicalism, see Randall Balmer, *Mine Eyes Have Seen the Glory: A Journey into the Evangelical Subculture in America,* 4th ed. (New York: Oxford University Press, 2006), esp. xiii–xvi. Cf. Randall Balmer, *Encyclopedia of Evangelicalism,* rev. ed. (Waco, TX: Baylor University Press, 2004).

an adult, rather than in infancy, as a public attestation to one's conversion.[3]

Following his baptism and his matriculation at the United States Naval Academy, Carter taught Sunday school to the children of officers and enlisted men stationed in Annapolis. On occasion, he conducted worship services when he was on board ships and submarines. The death of Carter's father in 1953 prompted the naval officer to resign his commission in order to return home and run the family's peanut business. There he resumed his Sunday school teaching at Plains Baptist Church.

After the United States Supreme Court issued its landmark *Brown v. Board of Education* decision on May 17, 1954, which mandated the desegregation of public schools, Carter emerged as a voice of moderation calling for racial tolerance in a county considered a stronghold of the John Birch Society. When the Plains chapter of the White Citizens' Council asked the now successful businessman to become a member of their segregationist organization, Carter refused. When a follow-up group of men showed up at the Carter warehouse and offered to pay Carter's five-dollar dues to join the organization, he pulled a five-dollar bill from his company's cash register and informed the delegation, "I'll take this and flush it down the toilet, but I am not going to join the White Citizens' Council."[4]

By 1962 Carter, already chair of the Sumter County school board, began looking for additional ways to serve the commu-

---

3. My narrative account of Carter's childhood and early career owes a great deal to Pippert, *Spiritual Journey of Jimmy Carter.*

4. Jimmy Carter, *Turning Point: A Candidate, a State, and a Nation Come of Age* (New York: Times Books, 1992), 21, 23.

nity. On October 1, 1962, his thirty-eighth birthday, Carter announced his candidacy for the Democratic nomination for state
senate; he later insisted that he had no thoughts at the time about
seeking higher office. When, in the course of the campaign, a visiting evangelist chastised him for running for elective office rather
than entering the ministry or some kind of social-service work,
Carter responded that he believed that public service was itself a
ministry. "How would you like to be the pastor of a church with
eighty thousand members?" he asked rhetorically.[5]

Carter campaigned hard for the seat, taking time away from
the family business whenever he could to make phone calls, knock
on doors, or visit radio stations. His reputation for being "soft" on
segregation proved to be an impediment for many of the district's
voters, especially in rural areas, but others recognized his character. "Jimmy Carter has shown his courage of conviction and stood
for what he considered right, sometimes in the face of strong opposition among his own people, and still retained their respect
and friendship," the *Americus Times-Recorder* wrote in lending its
endorsement. "This is an important attribute for a man in public
office, since win or lose, he must retain the respect and confidence of his constituents."[6]

"I was a naïve thirty-eight-year-old farmer and small-town
businessman," Carter recounted in *Turning Point,* his recollection
of that pivotal campaign. "I confronted forces of electoral fraud
and corruption that are almost unimaginable today." The initial
returns indicated that Carter had been narrowly defeated. On
election day, Carter and some of his supporters had witnessed

---

5. Carter, *Turning Point,* 63.

6. Quoted in Carter, *Turning Point,* 72.

massive, even shameless, voter fraud in Quitman County, where even the deceased voted in alphabetical order—and invariably for Carter's opponent.[7]

With typical pluck and determination, and armed with a conviction of the moral rectitude of his case—"I had been betrayed by a political system in which I had confidence, and I was mad as hell!"—Carter demanded redress. Assisted by the glare of publicity from the *Atlanta Journal* and other news organizations, many of them eager to expose the corruption of county bosses in Georgia, Carter won the opportunity for another plebiscite. He prevailed and took the oath of office as a state senator in January 1963.[8]

Following his reelection two years later, Carter decided to seek the Democratic nomination for governor. This time he was defeated, and the loss was especially disappointing because the victor was the notorious arch-segregationist Lester Maddox. When three African Americans had sought to integrate his Pickrick Cafeteria in Atlanta on the day after the Civil Rights Act of 1964 was signed into law, Maddox brandished a pistol and told them to leave. He yelled, "You no good dirty devils! You dirty Communists!" Several patrons, wielding axe handles, helped Maddox turn the potential customers away.

For Carter, losing to a man who enjoyed the support of the Ku Klux Klan was a bitter defeat. When George C. Wallace of Alabama had lost his bid for the Democratic gubernatorial nomination to a rabid segregationist in 1958, he famously vowed (in a phrase just as offensive today as it was then) that he would "never be out-

---

7. Carter, *Turning Point*, xix.

8. Carter, *Turning Point*, 100.

niggered again." When Jimmy Carter lost his bid for the governor-ship to Maddox in 1966, it prompted a great deal of soul-searching and even spiritual renewal in the politician from Plains, Georgia.

He sought spiritual counsel from his sister Ruth Carter Stapleton, an evangelist. About this time, Carter remembered hearing a sermon entitled, "If you were arrested for being a Christian, would there be enough evidence to convict you?" He took the challenge to heart. "I never had really committed myself totally to God," he told Bill Moyers in 1976. "My Christian beliefs were superficial. Based primarily on pride and—I'd never done much for other people. I was always thinking about myself, and I changed somewhat for the better. I formed a much more intimate relationship with Christ. And, since then, I've had just about a new life."[9]

Carter embarked on several short-term missionary assignments, the first for a week-long sortie in Massachusetts with a Cuban pastor who specialized in outreach to Spanish-speaking people. In 1968 Carter, together with five other Southern Baptist laymen, canvassed neighborhoods in the town of Lock Haven, Pennsylvania, talking to residents about Jesus and sharing their faith. The experience was transformative. He later recalled that during his time in Lock Haven he had felt "closest to Christ and first experienced in a personal and intense way the presence of the Holy Spirit in my life."[10]

When Carter tried again for the governorship of Georgia in 1970, he was successful, winning 59 percent of the vote. Though

---

9. Quoted in Pippert, *Spiritual Journey of Jimmy Carter,* 5, 6.

10. Quoted in Pippert, *Spiritual Journey of Jimmy Carter,* 6. In my only meeting with Carter, in a small group prior to an event at Emory University, he talked almost exclusively about his experience in Lock Haven, recounting what a privilege it had been to be able to talk to others about Jesus.

he had campaigned for the statehouse as a conservative, Carter used the occasion of his inaugural address to announce that "the time for racial discrimination is over." He made good on his campaign promises to equalize state funding for rich and poor school districts, he appointed dozens of African Americans to hitherto all-white state boards and agencies, and he opened the capitol gallery to portraits of prominent Georgia blacks, starting with Martin Luther King Jr.

Shortly after his election as governor—and because, in part, he was limited to a single term—Carter and his staff began to explore the possibility of a run for the presidency. Carter had received some national attention as an example of the "New South," a progressive-minded politician no longer constricted by the straightjacket of segregation. Still, his national profile was, to say the least, limited. At the chaotic Democratic National Convention of 1972, meeting in Miami Beach, Carter and his surrogates made a last-minute appeal to the staff of the presidential nominee, George S. McGovern, to suggest that Carter be considered for the vice-presidential slot. The Carter camp's phone calls went unreturned.[11]

Following McGovern's landslide defeat and the ensuing revelations about Watergate, Carter's candidacy for national office seemed a bit less improbable, but success was by no means assured. His name did not even appear in early public-opinion polls leading up to the 1976 primary season. Carter announced

---

11. Given McGovern's experience with his choice, Senator Thomas Eagleton of Missouri, Governor Carter would have been a far better option.

early—and virtually unnoticed—for the Democratic nomination, in December 1974, and then set about to conduct a vigorous
grassroots campaign in Iowa and New Hampshire. "Jimmy who?"
astounded the political pundits by winning nearly 28 percent of
the caucus votes in Iowa, more than twice the tally of his near-
est challenger. Several weeks later he won the first-in-the-nation
Democratic primary in New Hampshire.

The large number of liberal candidates—Birch Bayh of Indiana, Fred Harris of Oklahoma, Morris Udall of Arizona—effectively neutralized one another, to Carter's advantage. But Carter's
singular accomplishment in the Democratic primaries was to
defeat George Wallace in Florida, Indiana, and North Carolina.
Wallace had mounted an independent bid for the presidency in
1968, and he had been paralyzed by a would-be assassin's bullet
while campaigning for the Democratic nomination in Maryland
in 1972. Many Democrats feared Wallace's populist appeal, but
Carter's ability to dispatch the Alabama segregationist had the
double advantage of saving the Democratic Party from embar-
rassment and also of offering a moderate, "New South" candidate
to the American voters.

Following his acceptance speech at the Democratic National-
al Convention in New York City, Carter and his running mate,
Senator Walter F. Mondale of Minnesota, stood arm-in-arm on
the dais with a stunning array of unlikely allies. Jesse Jackson,
Andrew Young, and Coretta Scott King, widow of the slain civil-
rights leader, stood with Wallace, the wheelchair-bound segregationist, as all sang the anthem of the civil-rights era, "We Shall
Overcome." Eugene McCarthy, whose followers had been crushed
by the Chicago police at the 1968 Democratic National Convention, stood with Richard J. Daley, the mayor of Chicago who had

ordered the crackdown against the antiwar protesters. "Everyone in the room wept," one reporter recalled as he recounted the extraordinary tableaux in Madison Square Garden. "Everyone in the room—even in the press section—linked arms and swayed back and forth and sang. It was a moment of healing that carried tremendous emotional power."[12]

Before Carter could deliver on his pledge to restore goodness and integrity to the Oval Office, however, he had to defeat the Republican nominee. After a bruising primary season and a cliffhanger Republican National Convention, Gerald R. Ford finally vanquished his primary opponent, Ronald Reagan, the former governor of California. Ford began the fall campaign with a massive disadvantage in popular opinion, more than a 30 percent deficit, according to some polls, but he steadily gained in popularity throughout the campaign.

Ford's task was complicated by his unpopular pardon of Richard Nixon and by the fact that Carter had so effectively staked out the issues of morality and probity in the post-Watergate era. Ford, however, was not without his claims to faith. A devout Episcopal layman, Ford was a man of considerable piety. His son Michael was a divinity student at an evangelical school, Gordon-Conwell Theological Seminary, in Massachusetts. But Ford expressed reluctance to play the "faith card" during the campaign. "I have always felt a closeness to God and have looked to a higher

---

12. Hendrick Hertzberg, "Jimmy Carter, 1977–1981," in *Character Above All: Ten Presidents from FDR to George Bush,* ed. Robert A. Wilson (New York: Simon & Schuster, 1995), 182.

being for guidance and support," he explained, "but I didn't think it was appropriate to advertise my religious beliefs."[13]

Ford's attempts to counter Carter's religiosity doubtless were hampered by his campaign's ham-handed analysis of American religious life, one that owed more to H. L. Mencken's shopworn stereotypes of the 1920s than to any sophisticated sociological study. "Roughly the denominations divide among the doctrinally more conservative, though politically more liberal, so called 'main line' groups, such as Episcopalians and Presbyterians; and the more evangelical fundamentalists, such as Baptists; with Methodists and Lutherans, two very important groups falling somewhere in between," a campaign strategy book read. "The main-line groups are more common in metropolitan areas and small cities, while the fundamentalists are more common in rural areas and small towns; but both are found in both geographic areas." The campaign strategy book urged Ford to attack Carter "as one who uses religion for political purposes; an evangelic [sic]."[14]

Ford did not help himself when, in the course of the second of three presidential debates, he declared that Eastern Europe was free of Soviet domination. Carter himself stumbled when he agreed to sit for an interview with *Playboy* magazine. The bulk of the interview itself was unremarkable—aside from its venue, sandwiched among pages of beautiful, naked women. Carter talked about his background and his experience as governor of Georgia, and he affirmed the traditional Baptist understandings

13. Quoted in Nancy Gibbs and Michael Duffy, "The Other Born-again President," *Time,* January 15, 2007, 41.

14. Notebook, Campaign Strategy for President Ford 1976 [loose-leaf notebook], Gerald R. Ford Library.

of the configuration of church and state. "The reason the Baptist Church was formed in this country," he told the interviewer, "was because of our belief in absolute and total separation of church and state."[15]

The conversation turned inevitably to Carter's faith. "Committing adultery, according to the Bible—which I believe in—is a sin," the candidate said. "For us to hate one another, for us to have sexual intercourse outside marriage, for us to engage in homosexual activities, for us to steal, for us to lie—these are all sins. But Jesus teaches us not to judge other people. We don't assume the role of judge and say to another human being, 'You're condemned because you commit sins.' All Christians, all of us, acknowledge that we are sinful and the judgment comes from God, not from another human being."[16]

All of this was standard evangelical fare. Toward the end of the interview, the candidate became expansive. "I try not to commit a deliberate sin," Carter declared. "Christ said, 'I tell you that anyone who looks on a woman with lust has in his heart already committed adultery.' I've looked on a lot of women with lust. I've committed adultery in my heart many times." Again, no evangelical would find this statement exceptional. "This is something that God recognizes I will do—and I have done it—and God forgives me for it," Carter continued, careful once again to insist that he was not superior to other sinners. "But that doesn't mean that I condemn someone who not only looks on a woman with lust but who leaves his wife and shacks up with somebody out of wedlock. Christ says, Don't consider yourself better than someone else be-

15. "*Playboy* Interview: Jimmy Carter," *Playboy*, November 1976, 86.

16. "*Playboy* Interview," 68.

cause one guy screws a whole bunch of women while the other guy is loyal to his wife. The guy who's loyal to his wife ought not to be condescending or proud because of the relative degree of sinfulness."[17]

"I don't think I would ever take the same frame of mind that Nixon or Johnson did—lying, cheating and distorting the truth," Carter concluded. "I think that my religious beliefs alone would prevent that from happening."[18]

By the time the November 1976 issue of *Playboy* hit the news-stands, Carter's candid admissions were treated as sensational, especially amid an otherwise dreary campaign. Pundits regarded Carter's comments as risible; an editorial cartoonist depicted the candidate leering at the Statue of Liberty. Although most evangelicals themselves found nothing egregious in the gist of Carter's comments, many were less than happy with his choice of language, like the word *screw*. Carter's own pastor, Bruce Edwards, lamented, "I do wish he had used different words."[19]

Other evangelical leaders, already looking for an opportunity to discredit Carter and move more decisively in the direction of the Republican Party, were less forgiving about the *Playboy* interview. "I am highly offended by this," W. A. Criswell, the Southern Baptist pastor of First Baptist Church in Dallas, Texas, declared. "I think he's mixed up in his moral values, and I think the entire church membership will feel the same way. The whole thing is highly distasteful." Another Southern Baptist

---

17. "*Playboy* Interview," 86.

18. "*Playboy* Interview," 86.

19. Quoted in Jules Witcover, *Marathon: The Pursuit of the Presidency, 1972–1976* (New York: Viking, 1977), 567.

minister, representing the advance guard of what would in the ensuing years become the Religious Right, criticized Carter for submitting to an interview in a magazine he regarded as pornographic. "*Playboy* is known for its gutter approach to life," Jerry Vines, a prominent minister from Mobile, Alabama, said. "A lot of us are not convinced that Mr. Carter is truly in the evangelical Christian camp."[20]

Carter, however, survived the *Playboy* fiasco. On November 2, 1976, the former governor of Georgia prevailed with 50.1 percent of the popular vote to Ford's 48.0 percent. "I believe that you will go down in history as one of America's great Presidents," Billy Graham wrote to Ford in consolation. "You are admired, loved and appreciated."[21]

Immediately after Jimmy Carter took the oath of office on January 20, 1977, he directed his first public words as president to Gerald Ford, the man he had defeated the previous November. "For myself and for our Nation," Carter said, "I want to thank my predecessor for all he has done to heal our land." The new president talked about "the inner and spiritual strength of our Nation" and called for a government that would be "both competent and compassionate." The Sunday school teacher from Plains, Georgia, recalled the words of Micah, the Hebrew prophet, who chastised ancient Israel for its complacency and for its refusal to act with justice. Then Carter set out an agenda: "Our commitment to hu-

---

20. Quoted in Witcover, *Marathon*, 567, 568.

21. Letter, Billy Graham to Gerald R. Ford, November 24, 1976, Name Files, White House Central Files, Gerald R. Ford Library.

man rights must be absolute, our laws fair, our national beauty preserved; the powerful must not persecute the weak, and human dignity must be enhanced."[22]

Carter busied himself to accomplish those goals. At a considerable cost of political capital, especially early in his administration, he completed a renegotiation of the Panama Canal treaties, the effect of which was to turn the canal over to the Panamanians. Although this project had been initiated by the Ford administration, Carter thought it was the right thing to do, especially if the United States hoped to improve relationships with Latin American countries. Carter characterized the new treaty as "a gracious apology" for "past wrongdoing." As no president before him or since, Carter began to emphasize the importance of human rights, even though such preachments angered some allies. "The basic thrust of human affairs points toward a more universal demand for fundamental human rights," Carter told the United Nations early in his presidency. "The United States has a historical birthright to be associated with this process."[23]

While Carter believed that he was pursuing an agenda guided by moral, Christian principles, other evangelicals, including many fellow Baptists, were already plotting to undermine him. Although leaders of the Religious Right would try to argue in later decades that the United States Supreme Court's

22. John Woolley and Gerhard Peters, *The American Presidency Project* [online]. Santa Barbara, CA: University of California (hosted), Gerhard Peters (database). http://www.presidency.ucsb.edu/ws/?pid=6575.

23. Quoted in Gary Scott Smith, *Faith and the Presidency: From George Washington to George W. Bush* (New York: Oxford Univ. Press, 2006), 315; John Woolley and Gerhard Peters, *The American Presidency Project* [online]. Santa Barbara, CA: University of California (hosted), Gerhard Peters (database). http://www.presidency.ucsb.edu/ws/?pid=7183.

1973 *Roe v. Wade* decision was the catalyst behind their political activism, that claim collapses beneath historical scrutiny. As early as the 1972 Iowa precinct caucuses, the Roman Catholic Church had been counseling Catholics to support candidates opposed to abortion, but evangelicals took a different view of the matter. Meeting in St. Louis during the summer of 1971, the "messengers" (delegates) to the Southern Baptist Convention passed a resolution that stated, "we call upon Southern Baptists to work for legislation that will allow the possibility of abortion under such conditions as rape, incest, clear evidence of severe fetal deformity, and carefully ascertained evidence of the likelihood of damage to the emotional, mental, and physical health of the mother." The Southern Baptist Convention reaffirmed that position in 1974 and again in 1976.[24]

Shortly after the *Roe* decision was handed down on January 22, 1973, W. A. Criswell, former president of the Southern Baptist Convention and pastor of First Baptist Church in Dallas, expressed his satisfaction with the ruling. "I have always felt that it was only after a child was born and had a life separate from its mother that it became an individual person," one of the most famous fundamentalists of the twentieth century declared, "and it has always, therefore, seemed to me that what is best for the mother and for the future should be allowed."[25]

While a few evangelical voices, including *Christianity Today* magazine, registered mild dissent over the *Roe* decision, the

---

24. *Annual of the Southern Baptist Convention* (Nashville, TN: Executive Committee, Southern Baptist Convention, 1971), 72.

25. Quoted in "What Price Abortion?" *Christianity Today*, March 2, 1975, 39 [565].

overwhelming response on the part of evangelicals was silence, even approval; Baptists, in particular, applauded the decision as an appropriate articulation of the line of division between church and state, between personal morality and state regulation of individual behavior. "Religious liberty, human equality and justice are advanced by the Supreme Court abortion decision," W. Barry Garrett of *Baptist Press* wrote.[26]

If the *Roe* decision was not the precipitating cause for the rise of the Religious Right, however, what was? The catalyst for the Religious Right was indeed a court decision, but it was a lower court decision, *Green v. Connally,* not *Roe v. Wade.* In the early 1970s, the federal government was looking for ways to extend the provisions of the Civil Rights Act of 1964, the landmark legislation that Lyndon Johnson pushed through Congress and signed into law on July 2, 1964. The Civil Rights Act forbade racial segregation and discrimination, and in looking for ways to enforce that law the Internal Revenue Service ruled that any organization that engaged in racial discrimination was not, by definition, a charitable organization. Therefore, such an institution should be denied tax-exempt status; furthermore, contributions to such organizations no longer qualified for tax-exemption.

On June 30, 1971, the three-judge District Court for the District of Columbia affirmed the IRS in its *Green v. Connally* decision. Although *Green v. Connally* addressed the case of a segregated school in Mississippi, the ramifications of the ruling were widespread. Institutions that engaged in racial discrimination, be they churches, clubs, or schools, could no longer lay claim to tax-exempt status.

---

26. Quoted in "What Price Abortion?" *Christianity Today.*

As the IRS prepared to apply the ruling, one of the schools directly in its crosshairs was a fundamentalist institution in Greenville, South Carolina: Bob Jones University. Founded in Florida by arch-fundamentalist Bob Jones in 1926, the school had been located for a time in Cleveland, Tennessee, before moving to South Carolina in 1947. In response to *Green v. Connally,* Bob Jones University decided to admit students of color in 1971, but the school maintained its restrictions against admitting unmarried African Americans until 1975. Even then, however, the school stipulated that interracial dating would be grounds for expulsion, and the school also promised that any students who "espouse, promote, or encourage others to violate the University's dating rules and regulations will be expelled."

The Internal Revenue Service pressed its case against Bob Jones University and on April 16, 1975, notified the school of the proposed revocation of its tax-exempt status. On January 19, 1976, the IRS officially revoked Bob Jones University's tax-exempt status, effective retroactively to 1970, when the school had first been formally notified of the IRS policy.

Bob Jones University sued to retain its tax exemption, and conservative activist Paul Weyrich saw an opening. Weyrich had been fighting for conservative causes going back to Barry Goldwater's failed bid for the presidency in 1964. He sensed the electoral potential of enlisting evangelical voters in conservative causes, and he had been trying throughout the early 1970s to generate some interest from evangelical leaders on matters like abortion, school prayer, and the proposed equal-rights amendment to the Constitution. "I was trying to get those people interested in those issues and I utterly failed," Weyrich recalled in 1990. "What changed their mind was Jimmy Carter's intervention against the

Christian schools, trying to deny them tax-exempt status on the basis of so-called de facto segregation."[27]

Despite appearances, the evangelical discontent over the IRS action against Bob Jones University was not principally about racism. Rather, evangelical leaders who banded together politically in the late 1970s saw themselves as defending the integrity of evangelical institutions against governmental interference. After the Scopes trial of 1925, evangelicals by and large had retreated into their own subculture of congregations, denominations, Bible camps and institutes, publishing houses, and the like—all of which they had constructed as a kind of alternative universe, free from the perceived corruptions of the larger culture. Evangelicals happily inhabited this subculture throughout the middle decades of the twentieth century, confident that they could carry on their activities without interference from the outside world.

Two court rulings, although separated by several decades, changed that. The Supreme Court's landmark *Brown v. Board of Education* decision of 1954, which mandated the desegregation of public schools, prompted many southerners to support—and to send their children to—what became know as segregation academies, many of them sponsored by religious organizations. Confident that First Amendment guarantees of the separation of church and state protected those institutions from government meddling, they paid little attention to the goings-on of the outside world. "Believing the Bible as I do," Jerry Falwell declared in 1965, "I would find it impossible to stop preaching

---

27. Quoted in William Martin, *With God on Our Side: The Rise of the Religious Right in America* (New York: Broadway Books, 1996), 173.

the pure saving gospel of Jesus Christ, and begin doing anything else—including fighting communism, or participating in civil-rights reforms."[28]

Although generalizations about the vast and internally diverse movement that is American evangelicalism are always perilous, Falwell's sentiments were not all that unusual. While they occasionally railed again "godless communism" during the throes of the Cold War, America's evangelicals were content, by and large, to remain cosseted within their own subculture. Many of them didn't bother to vote, and many others were not even registered.

Carter's campaign for the presidency, and his declaration that he was a "born again" Christian, caught the attention many evangelicals, Southerners especially. But those who turned out to vote for the Democratic candidate in the 1976 presidential election were by no means part of an orchestrated political movement. Most evangelicals, and their leaders, remained un-politicized.

*Green v. Connally* changed that. Evangelical leaders, prodded by Weyrich, chose to interpret the IRS ruling against segregation-ist schools as an assault on the integrity and the sanctity of the evangelical subculture. And that is what prompted them to action and to organize into a political movement. "What caused the movement to surface," Weyrich reiterated, "was the federal government's moves against the Christian schools," which, he added, "enraged the Christian community." Weyrich was just as emphatic about what did not motivate evangelical leaders. The catalyst for

---

28. Quoted in Frances Fitzgerald, *Cities on a Hill: A Journey Through Contemporary American Cultures* (New York: Simon & Schuster, 1981), 29.

evangelical political activism, he insisted in 1990, "was not the school-prayer issue, and it was not the abortion issue."[29]

Ed Dobson, formerly Falwell's assistant at Moral Majority, has corroborated Weyrich's account. "The Religious New Right did not start because of a concern about abortion," he said. "I sat in the non-smoke-filled back room with the Moral Majority, and I frankly do not remember abortion being mentioned as a reason why we ought to do something." In the same comments, Dobson cited "government interference in Christian schools" as one of the reasons for the founding of the Religious Right and noted that this movement, minted in the late 1970s, "attempted to preserve the integrity of our organizations."[30]

The Bob Jones case found its way all the way to the Supreme Court in 1982, when the Reagan administration argued on behalf of Bob Jones University. On May 24, 1983, however, the Court ruled against Bob Jones (William Rehnquist, later appointed chief justice, was the lone dissenter). The evangelical defense of Bob Jones University and its racially discriminatory policies may not have been motivated primarily by racism. Still, it's fair to point out the paradox that the very people who styled themselves the "new abolitionists" to emphasize their moral kinship with the nineteenth-century opponents of slavery actually coalesced as a political movement, effectively, to defend racial discrimination.

And how did opposition to abortion come under the purview of the Religious Right? According to Weyrich, once these

---

29. Michael Cromartie, ed., *No Longer Exiles: The Religious New Right in American Politics* (Washington, DC: Ethics and Public Policy Center, 1993), 25–26.

30. Cromartie, *No Longer Exiles*, 52.

evangelical leaders had mobilized in defense of Bob Jones University, they held a conference call to discuss the prospect of other, wider political involvement. Several people suggested possible issues, and finally a voice on the end of one of the lines said, "How about abortion?" And that, according to Weyrich, was how abortion was cobbled into the agenda of the Religious Right—in the late 1970s, not as a direct response to the January 1973 *Roe v. Wade* decision.[31]

Another element of Paul Weyrich's statement merits closer examination. Looking back on the formation of the Religious Right, Weyrich insisted that opposition to abortion was not the precipitating cause behind evangelical political activism. His alternate explanation reads as follows: "What changed their mind was Jimmy Carter's intervention against the Christian schools, trying to deny them tax-exempt status on the basis of so-called de facto segregation."[32]

Here, Weyrich displayed his genius for political maneuvering and chicanery. The Internal Revenue Service had initiated its action against Bob Jones University in 1970, and the agency informed the school in 1975 that it would revoke its tax exemption, which was finally done on January 19, 1976. Jimmy Carter was still running for the Democratic nomination when Bob Jones University received that news, and he was inaugurated president on January 20, 1977, precisely one full year and a day *after* the IRS finally rescinded the school's tax-exempt status. And yet, according to

31. I address this debate over the origins of the Religious Right, what I call the "abortion myth," more fully in *Thy Kingdom Come: How the Religious Right Distorts the Faith and Threatens America* (New York: Basic Books, 2006), chap. 1.

32. Quoted in Martin, *With God on Our Side,* 173.

Weyrich, it was "Jimmy Carter's intervention against the Christian schools" that precipitated the rise of the Religious Right.[33]

As president of the United States in the final years of the 1970s, Carter was dealt a bad hand—the Arab Oil Embargo and the concomitant energy crisis, high interest rates, the Iranian hostage situation—and it is a hand that, in many respects, he played badly. But he also fought against some lavishly funded, highly organized, and fiendishly deceptive opponents who would do almost anything to undermine him. Weyrich's attribution to Carter of the IRS action against Bob Jones University provides a case in point. Even though the action was consummated a full year before Carter even took office, when Gerald Ford was still president, Weyrich succeeded in pinning this unpopular action on the Democratic president and using it to organize a movement to deny him reelection in 1980.

Another religious development, concomitant with the rise of the Religious Right, would have a profound effect on the American political landscape in ensuing decades. In 1979, conservatives, led by Paige Patterson and Paul Pressler, orchestrated a takeover of the Sothern Baptist Convention. At issue, according to conservatives in the denomination, was the denomination's perceived slide into liberalism. Patterson and Pressler sought to arrest what they considered a decline, and they devised an ingenious way to do so.

In studying the constitution and by-laws of the Southern Baptist Convention, Pressler and Patterson noted the broad appointive powers assigned to the denomination's president, who is

---

33. Quoted in Martin, *With God on Our Side,* 173.

elected every year by the "messengers" (delegates) to the annual convention. If only the denomination's conservatives could elect a succession of like-minded presidents, those men (invariably men) could in turn appoint other conservatives to denominational agencies and, more important, to the boards of various Southern Baptist colleges and seminaries.

That is precisely what Patterson and Pressler, in league with other conservatives, set out to do. For months leading up to the Southern Baptist meeting in June 1979, they organized a grass-roots campaign to send conservative messengers to the convention. On June 12, 1979, their efforts paid off; amid charges of voting irregularities and political maneuvering, the Southern Baptists elected Adrian Rogers, pastor of Bellevue Baptist Church in Memphis, Tennessee, as president of the denomination. Rogers, addressing the Baptist Pastors' Association, praised "conservative, Bible-believing" congregations that "believe in the inerrant, infallible word of God."[34]

Although many Southern Baptists and other observers have questioned the supposed presence of "liberalism" within the denomination—the term *liberal Southern Baptist* seems oxymoronic—the conservatives, who were often labeled fundamentalists by their opponents, believed otherwise. Beginning with Rogers's election in 1979, and continuing in an unbroken line to the present, the Southern Baptist Convention has been headed by theologically—and politically—conservative presidents. These men have appointed other conservatives to denominational boards

---

34. Quoted in George Vecsey, "Southern Baptists Choose a Conservative President," *New York Times,* June 13, 1979. Regarding the claims of electioneering, see George Vecsey, "Official of Southern Baptists Plans Inquiry on New President's Election," *New York Times,* June 16, 1979.

and agencies and have, their critics charged, imposed a kind of litmus test on matters ranging from political conservativism to biblical "inerrancy" and opposition to the ordination of women.

These appointees to various agencies and boards, in turn, sought to purge the Southern Baptist Convention and its affiliated organizations of those they considered liberals—though "liberals" prefer the designation *moderates*. The effect of these purges has been wrenching, not only for those who lost their jobs—at Southern Baptist Theological Seminary, for instance, one of the fiercest battlefields of the takeover—but also for grassroots Southern Baptists, many of whom believed that the conservatives had commandeered their church.[35]

The conservative takeover of the Southern Baptist Convention, however, had reverberations in the political arena as well. Throughout American history, going back to the 1630s, Baptists have been insistent defenders of liberty of conscience and the separation of church and state. The notion that the church should not seek the imprimatur of the state is a Baptist idea, originating with Roger Williams. Throughout American history, Baptists have always been stalwart defenders of church-state separation.

The Baptist tradition of defending the autonomy of the church from the state and the state from the church, however, was another casualty of the conservative takeover of the Southern Baptist Convention in 1979. The conservatives who took charge of the denomination quickly demonstrated that they had little interest in patrolling Roger Williams's "wall of separation."

35. For an account of these changes in the Southern Baptist Convention, see Nancy Tatom Ammerman, *Baptist Battles: Social Change and Religious Conflict in the Southern Baptist Convention* (New Brunswick, NJ: Rutgers University Press, 1990).

They sought instead to compromise, and eventually to obliterate, the provisions of the First Amendment. Adrian Rogers, the pastor elected president of the Southern Baptist Convention in 1979, for instance, was one of the speakers at a massive Religious Right rally in the course of the 1980 presidential campaign where Ronald Reagan articulated his narrow, pointedly unilateral understanding of the First Amendment. "The First Amendment was written not to protect the people and their laws from religious values," Reagan said, "but to protect those values from government tyranny."[36]

Other conservative Southern Baptists would go even further. In 1960 W. A. Criswell had declared that "it is written in our country's constitution that church and state must be, in this nation, forever separate and free." In the Reagan era, however, Criswell changed his tune. "I believe this notion of the separation of church and state was the figment of some infidel's imagination," he said.[37]

One of the many ironies surrounding the Religious Right, of course, is that evangelicals, including many Southern Baptists, had helped sweep Carter, a Southern Baptist, to victory in the presidential election of 1976. His rhetoric about being a "born again" Christian had energized evangelicals, many of whom had been resolutely apolitical until the mid-1970s. His dark-horse run for the presidency, his candor about his religious convictions, and his promise to restore probity to the White House resonated with

---

36. Quoted in Howell Raines, "Reagan Backs Evangelicals in Their Political Activities," *New York Times,* August 23, 1980.

37. Quoted in Richard V. Pierard, "Civil Religion: A Case Study Showing How Some Baptists Went Astray on the Separation of Church and State," *Christian Ethics Today,* 8 (November 1996).

many Americans, especially after having endured Richard Nixon's endless deceits. Many evangelicals registered to vote for the first time in order to cast their ballots for the Southern Baptist Sunday school teacher from Georgia, and even televangelist Pat Robertson later boasted that he had done everything short of violating FCC regulations to ensure Carter's election.

Not all evangelicals were enthusiastic about Carter, however. Tim LaHaye insisted that he had been suspicious from the beginning. Once they had coalesced into a political movement, leaders of the Religious Right claimed that Carter's unwillingness to outlaw abortion provided a compelling reason to work against him; Carter had taken the position during the 1976 campaign that he was "personally opposed" to abortion but that he did not want to make it illegal. But that was a retrospective judgment because evangelicals did not embrace abortion as a political issue until after the 1976 campaign.

Once politically conservative evangelical leaders decided to organize, in advance of the 1980 election, they were able to tap into a reservoir of popular discontent. Many Americans had felt the seismic changes in their society over the course of the twentieth century. Divorce rates were on the rise. Changes to the immigration laws in 1965 had begun to recast the ethnic composition as well as the religious landscape in America; one consequence was that American Protestants, while certainly still a majority, no longer enjoyed the hegemonic status they once enjoyed—or thought they did.

Many conservatives had decried the Supreme Court's school-prayer decisions of the early 1960s, which they erroneously caricatured as outlawing prayer in public schools. The Court did no such thing—as long as there are algebra tests, students will pray in public schools!—but the Court stepped in and ruled that prescribed public prayers in public schools violated the First Amendment. The issue had festered among conservatives, including many evangelicals, for some time. The architects of the Religious Right in the late 1970s folded promises to "restore" prayer in public schools into their agenda.

What about other issues that fed the rise of the Religious Right? Phyllis Schlafly, a Roman Catholic, had been opposing the proposed equal-rights amendment to the United States Constitution, but the issue had little traction among evangelicals in the early 1970s. As the Religious Right was gearing up in preparation for the 1980 election, however, Beverly LaHaye started a new organization, Concerned Women for America, in 1979, claiming that she resented the assumption on the part of feminist leaders that they spoke for all women.

As the 1980 presidential election approached, Carter faced daunting obstacles in his quest for reelection: the energy crisis, the Iranian hostage situation, record-high interest rates, and dwindling personal popularity. The incumbent president was forced to turn back a primary challenge from Senator Edward Kennedy of Massachusetts. But Carter also faced a determined band of conservative operatives who had cleverly mobilized many evangelical leaders into an unaccustomed posture of political activism. Jerry Falwell founded Moral Majority in 1979, and a slew of other organizations—Religious Roundtable, Traditional Values Coalition, Concerned Women for America—galvanized to become a formidable political movement popularly known as the Religious Right.

Carter, at least to some degree, played into the hands of the Religious Right. In the course of the 1976 campaign, he had promised to convene a White House conference that would address the concerns of families. Distracted by his other obligations, however—the hostages in Iran, the energy crisis, his personal diplomacy to bring peace to the Middle East, which culminated in the Camp David accords—Carter had placed the conference on hold. As the 1980 election approached, he felt obligated to redeem his promise and delegated the responsibility for organizing the conference to surrogates. When the White House Conference on Families opened in Baltimore on June 5, 1980, it became apparent that conference planners had taken a rather broad view of what constituted a family, including single-parent families and same-sex parents.

Leaders of the Religious Right pounced on yet another reason to defeat the Southern Baptist incumbent. The term "family values" would become a mantra for religious conservatives in the years ahead, even though their embrace of the phrase required a deft sleight of hand in advance of the fall election.

Jerry Falwell, shown here with Ronald Reagan in Lynchburg, Virginia, a month before the 1980 presidential election, helped to organize evangelicals into a potent political force. Evangelicals' embrace of Reagan, a divorced and remarried man who had signed into law a bill legalizing abortion, required some deft maneuvering by Falwell and other leaders of the Religious Right.

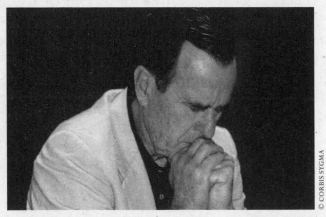

George H. W. Bush, then vice president and running for president, prays for the victims of Hurricane Andrew in 1992. Bush, an Episcopalian, drew support from the Religious Right, though many evangelicals remained suspicious of his sudden "conversion" to a "pro-life" position when Ronald Reagan tapped him to be vice president in 1980.

# FOUR

# LISTING RIGHT

*Ronald Reagan, George Bush, and the "Evil Empire"*

On the cover of their October 25, 1976, issue, the editors of
*Newsweek* anointed 1976 "The Year of the Evangelical." That designation, however, may have been four years premature. For evangelical Christians, many of whom were still politically quiescent
well into the 1970s, the year 1976 had indeed been extraordinary: Charles Colson, the former Watergate felon, had published
a best-selling memoir called *Born Again,* and a Southern Baptist
Sunday school teacher, Jimmy Carter, rose from political obscurity to win election to the presidency.

By evangelical standards, however, the 1980 presidential
election was even more significant. All three of the major candidates for president claimed to be evangelical Christians. Carter,
of course, had established his "born again" credentials during the
1976 campaign. John B. Anderson, Republican congressman from
Illinois running as an independent, was a member of the Evangelical Free Church of America; in 1964 Anderson had been named

"Layman of the Year" by the National Association of Evangelicals. The Republican nominee, Ronald Reagan, former governor of California, also claimed to be an evangelical Christian.

The rise of the Religious Right in the late 1970s had utterly transformed the electoral landscape in advance of the 1980 election. Carter, who had won 56 percent of the white Baptist vote in the South in 1976, could no longer count on the support of white evangelicals. Anderson, arguably more liberal than either Carter or Reagan, made a bid for evangelical voters, although his support for abortion rights incurred the wrath of evangelicals newly attuned to that issue. Though on the face of it Reagan had the weakest claim to evangelical faith, given the fact that he was a divorced and remarried man who rarely attended church, he was able to harvest a majority of evangelical votes, enough to propel him to victory in the November election.

Ronald Reagan was born to John Edward "Jack" Reagan, a shoe salesman and a Roman Catholic, and to Nelle Wilson Reagan, a Protestant. Jack Reagan, an alcoholic, was nevertheless a man of principle. He refused to take his children to see *The Birth of a Nation,* the motion picture that glorified the Ku Klux Klan, and he walked out of a hotel and slept in his car rather than patronize an establishment that excluded Jews. Until the family settled in Dixon, Illinois, when Ronald was nine, the Reagans lived in various Illinois towns. Nelle Reagan reared her son in the Christian Church (Disciples of Christ), one of the denominations that arose out of the Restorationist movement at the beginning of the nineteenth century. "My mother gave me a great deal," Reagan recalled, but nothing more important than "the knowledge of the happiness and solace to be gained by talking to the Lord."[1]

Nelle Reagan took her children to Sunday school and to church, but she allowed them to decide whether to join. "At twelve," Ronald Reagan recalled in his autobiography, "I made my decision and was baptized as a member of the Disciples of Christ." The baptism took place on June 21, 1922, at the Disciples of Christ church in Dixon, Illinois.[2]

After graduating from high school, Reagan attended Eureka College, a Disciples of Christ school in Eureka, Illinois. He then landed a job as a sports announcer for WOC in Davenport, Iowa, which eventually folded into the larger, 50,000-watt station WHO in Des Moines. Reagan went to Hollywood in 1937, where he starred in B (for "budget") movies and in supporting roles in larger productions. Reagan, code-named T–10, was an informant for the FBI in the 1940s; he forwarded to the government the names of actors that he believed were communists. Reagan served two stints as president of the Screen Actors Guild, and in 1962 he formally changed his voter registration from Democratic to Republican.[3]

Two years later, during the final week of the Johnson-Goldwater presidential campaign, Reagan delivered a thirty-minute television speech on behalf of the Republican nominee. That

---

1. Quoted in Gary Scott Smith, *Faith and the Presidency: From George Washington to George W. Bush* (New York: Oxford University Press, 2006), 329. Lyndon Johnson was also a member of the Disciples of Christ.

2. Ronald Reagan, *An American Life* (New York: Simon & Schuster, 1990), 32; Smith, *Faith and the Presidency*, 326.

3. William A. DeGregorio, *The Complete Book of U.S. Presidents: From George Washington to George W. Bush,* rev. ed. (New York: Barnes & Noble, 2004), 641.

speech, according to the *New York Times,* produced more political contributions than any other political speech in history. Reagan then embarked on his own political career, winning election as governor of California in 1966.[4]

In 1940, near the beginning of his career as an actor, Reagan had married an actress, Jane Wyman, whom he had met during the filming of *Brother Rat* in 1938. A decade later, however, as Wyman's career was flourishing—she won an Oscar for best actress in 1948—and Reagan's was stagnant, at least by comparison, the marriage began to fray. Reagan and Wyman divorced in 1948. The court awarded custody of the couple's two children to Wyman; a third child had died in infancy. In 1952 Reagan married another actress, Nancy Davis, whom he had met in 1949.[5]

As the newly organized Religious Right headed into the 1980 presidential campaign, its leaders faced something of a quandary. For decades, evangelical leaders had attached considerable stigma to divorce, and especially to remarriage after divorce while the first spouse was still living. The biblical warrant for this position was fairly clear. In the King James Version of Matthew 5:32, Jesus says that "whosoever shall put away his wife, saving for the cause of fornication, causeth her to commit adultery" and adds that "whosoever shall marry her that is divorced committeth adultery."

Among evangelicals, the prohibitions against divorce had been close to absolute throughout American history and for most

---

4. DeGregorio, *Complete Book,* 641.

5. Reagan's decade-long marriage to Wyman merits only two sentences in his autobiography. See Reagan, *American Life,* 92.

of the twentieth century. Anyone who was divorced faced likely expulsion from evangelical congregations, or at least ostracism—unless she (usually) or he was the aggrieved party. Through the 1970s, evangelical magazines such as *Christianity Today* regularly contained articles warning against the sin and the danger of divorce. By the 1980s, however, those admonitions about divorce dropped almost entirely from view.

What happened? Ironically, by the late 1970s the rate of divorce among evangelicals was virtually the same as that in the larger population. Churches had to deal more and more frequently with congregants who had been divorced. Evangelical leaders, therefore, many of them newly politicized, started to look for "sins" outside the evangelical community. The denunciations about divorce diminished; evangelical leaders began to emphasize abortion and, later, homosexuality—"sins" that they could safely identify outside evangelicalism, or so they thought.

The second reason for the sudden de-emphasis of divorce was political. In the run-up to the 1980 presidential campaign, the leaders of the Religious Right decided to anoint as their political savior a divorced and remarried man, Ronald Reagan.

But the embrace of Reagan by leaders of the Religious Right was complicated further by the fact that, as governor of California, Reagan had signed into law the Therapeutic Abortion Act of 1967, the nation's most permissive bill legalizing abortion. "I have never done more study on any one thing than the abortion bill," Reagan said in 1968. He later expressed regret for having signed the law, and by July 27, 1979, he had declared his support for a proposed Human Life Amendment: "I personally believe that interrupting a pregnancy is the taking of a human life and can be justified in self-defense, that is, if the mother's own life is in danger."[6]

Reagan's change of heart on abortion could be attributed to any number of factors. A less-than-charitable interpretation of Reagan's turnabout would be that he detected some political advantage in aligning himself with the "pro-life" movement in advance of the 1980 presidential campaign. Unfortunately, Reagan's autobiography, *An American Life,* provides no insight into his thinking on the matter. Despite the fact that Reagan repeatedly insisted that abortion ranked at or near the top of his moral concerns, despite his earlier support for legalized abortion, and despite his repeated promises to outlaw it as president, the subject of abortion appears nowhere in his 726-page autobiography.[7]

A more likely explanation for Reagan's turnabout is that he, along with many other Americans (including many evangelicals), was surprised, even horrified, at the rising number of abortions following the *Roe v. Wade* decision of 1973. Clearly, Reagan himself came to regret signing the California bill legalizing abortion, which had, in his own estimation, made possible more than a million abortions. Other Americans also became uneasy at the spike in abortions after 1973. At a meeting of the National Right to Life Committee in 1978, for instance, speakers talked about the

---

6. Quoted in Lou Cannon, *Reagan* (New York: G. P. Putnam's Sons, 1982), 129, 131. Cannon, Reagan's sympathetic biographer, points out that Reagan subsequently blamed physicians and psychiatrists for distorting the meaning of the bill by taking "advantage of a loophole in the bill of which he was not aware when he signed the measure." Cannon concludes, however: "This contention is hollow" (Cannon, *Reagan,* 131; cf. Lou Cannon, *President Reagan: The Role of a Lifetime* (New York: Simon & Schuster, 1991), 812.

7. Reagan, *American Life,* passim.

rising rate of abortions as a medical "holocaust." The president of the organization, Carolyn Gerter, vowed to work for the defeat of "pro-choice" members of Congress. "We are right and we are going to win," Gerter declared.[8]

And they did. The National Right to Life Committee made Senator Dick Clark, Democrat of Iowa, its number one target in the 1978 election; he lost his seat to Roger Jepsen, a "pro-life" candidate, a sign of the gathering strength of the "pro-life" movement. Those opposed to abortion distributed 300,000 pamphlets to churches across Iowa on the final Sunday before the election.[9]

The success of Jepsen's insurgent and underdog candidacy in 1978 provided the first real evidence that a growing number of grassroots evangelicals was becoming attuned to the abortion issue. The following year, evangelical theologian Francis Schaeffer teamed up with a pediatric surgeon, C. Everett Koop, to write a book, *Whatever Happened to the Human Race?,* a bitter lamentation about the *Roe* decision coupled with warnings that America would soon countenance infanticide and euthanasia. The book was accompanied by a five-part film, a series of illustrated lectures that toured the country and captured the attention of evangelicals. "The Protestants, and especially the evangelicals," Schaeffer wrote the following year, "have been so sluggish on this issue of human life, and *Whatever Happened to the Human Race?* is causing real waves, among church people and governmental people too." The evangelicals' new interest in the abortion issue, especially when combined

---

8. Nathaniel Sheppard Jr., "Group Fighting Abortion Planning to Step Up Its Drive," *New York Times,* July 3, 1978.

9. Douglas E. Kneeland, "Clark Defeat in Iowa Laid to Abortion Issue," *New York Times,* November 13, 1978.

with the long-standing "pro-life" sympathies of conservative Roman Catholics, made for a potentially powerful coalition.

Despite Reagan's apparent disqualifications, the leaders of the Religious Right were eager to designate the former governor of California as their political champion in the 1980 presidential campaign. This new conservative alliance willingly overlooked Reagan's earlier support for abortion and his status as a divorced and remarried man—a circumstance, by the way, that had prevented Nelson Rockefeller from receiving the support of evangelicals during his various runs at the Republican nomination in the 1960s.

The emergence of opposition to abortion as a litmus test for the Religious Right became evident in the reactions to the selection of George H. W. Bush as Reagan's running mate. Bush, formerly the head of the Central Intelligence Agency, had mounted a vigorous campaign for the Republican nomination as a "pro-choice" Republican and had derided Reagan's plan simultaneously to cut taxes and to increase military spending as "voodoo economics." When Reagan tapped him for vice president, however, Bush immediately changed his positions and defiantly informed reporters that he would not be "nickel-and-dimed" on these issues, meaning that he refused to answer for his sudden change of heart.[10]

The 1980 campaign unfolded beneath the cloud of the Iranian hostage situation, a moribund economy, and the Soviet invasion of Afghanistan in 1979—and all of those issues worked to the disadvantage of the incumbent president, Jimmy Carter.

---

10. Bush's father, Prescott Bush, was one of the founders of Planned Parenthood.

Leaders of the Religious Right, meanwhile, had been encouraging evangelicals to become registered voters, if they weren't already. And if those new voters wanted advice about how to cast their ballots, these Religious Right leaders were unstinting in their endorsement: Reagan was their man.

For his part, Reagan played to evangelical voters and, more generally, to people of faith. At the close of his acceptance speech at the Republican National Convention, for instance, the candidate asked, "Can we begin our crusade joined together in a moment of silent prayer?" Still, unlike Carter or (for that matter) Anderson, Reagan was not always fully conversant with the jargon of evangelicalism. During the campaign he told a reporter that his decision to join the Disciples of Christ church at age twelve represented a kind of conversion. "If that's what you mean by born-again," Reagan said, "you could call me born-again."[11]

As the campaign unfolded, it became clear early on that Reagan hoped to replicate Richard Nixon's "southern strategy" to pry white voters from the Democratic column, this despite the fact that the Democratic incumbent was a Southerner. To underscore his intentions, Reagan chose Philadelphia, Mississippi, where members of the Ku Klux Klan murdered three civil-rights workers on June 22, 1964, for his first campaign appearance after winning the Republican nomination. But in addition to white Southerners, Reagan also assiduously courted evangelical voters, another constituency that, four years earlier, had been partial to Carter.[12]

---

11. Quoted in Smith, *Faith and the Presidency,* 329, 336.

12. Douglas E. Kneeland, "Reagan Campaigns at Mississippi Fair," *New York Times,* August 4, 1980.

By the middle of August 1980, even the *New York Times,* often tone-deaf to the actions and the motivations of evangelicals, was taking notice of their political mobilization. "Abandoning a long-held belief that political activism is incompatible with their faith," John Herbers wrote, "ultraconservative evangelical Christians are forming a growing new force." Herbers noted that evangelicals had wrested control of the Republican Party in Alaska and that evangelicals in Iowa had bucked the more moderate Republican leaders and nominated "pro-life" conservatives. Evangelicals, he continued, "not only have added a new dimension and new members to the political right but also served as a kind of cement holding together the conservative single-issue groups in the name of family, basic morality and opposition to Government intervention."[13]

The turning point of the 1980 presidential campaign was arguably a gathering of politically conservative evangelicals in Dallas, Texas, on August 22. This meeting, called a "National Affairs Briefing," organized by a group called the Religious Roundtable, drew more than ten thousand evangelicals, including in excess of two thousand pastors. Preacher after stem-winding preacher addressed the audience, calling on the nation to repent of its sins: abortion and homosexuality. "I'm sick and tired of hearing about all of the radicals and the perverts and the liberals and the leftists and the Communists coming out of the closet," James Robison, a televangelist, said. "It's time for God's people to come out of the closet."[14]

---

13. John Herbers, "Ultraconservative Evangelicals a Surging New Force in Politics," *New York Times,* August 17, 1980.

14. Quoted in Howell Raines, "Reagan Backs Evangelicals in Their Political Activities," *New York Times,* August 23, 1980.

Although Carter and Anderson had both been invited to the meeting, both declined the invitation. Reagan, however, was there, having been coached extensively by Religious Right leaders about how to respond. After the succession of preachers, the Republican nominee approached the lectern. "I know this group can't endorse me," the candidate said, "but I want you to know that I endorse you and what you are doing." That comment, delivered with the impeccable timing of a seasoned actor, brought down the house, cemented the allegiance of politically conservative evangelicals to the Republican ticket, and probably decided the 1980 election. Reflecting on the outcome of the November balloting, Tim LaHaye, one of the Religious Right leaders, declared that God "saw thousands of us working diligently to awaken his sleeping church to its political responsibilities."[15]

Even before his inauguration on January 20, 1981, Reagan signaled that his choice for surgeon general would be C. Everett Koop, surgeon-in-chief at Children's Hospital in Philadelphia. Koop was an outspoken and passionate foe of abortion and coauthor, with Francis Schaeffer, of *Whatever Happened to the Human Race?*, the evangelical manifesto protesting the Supreme Court's *Roe v. Wade* decision.

Reagan appointed another evangelical, James G. Watt, to his cabinet as secretary of the interior. Watt, a member of the Assemblies of God, had been associated with the so-called Sagebrush

---

15. Quoted in Smith, *Faith and the Presidency,* 318, 319. In his Dallas speech, Reagan went on to declare that "Religious America is awakening ... perhaps just in time for our country's sake" (quoted in Raines, "Reagan Backs Evangelicals in Their Political Activities").

Rebellion, a coalition of western ranchers who wanted to open more wilderness areas to development and who opposed any efforts to alter their favorable grazing rights on federal lands. It was Watt who memorably conflated his responsibilities as interior secretary with his premillennialism, the doctrine that Jesus would return at any moment and the world would dissolve in apocalyptic judgment. "I do not know how many future generations we can count on before the Lord returns," Watt told stunned members of the House Interior Committee in February 1981. Although his ensuing statement, "Whatever it is, we have to manage with a skill to have the resources needed for future generations," was less widely reported, critics contended that his policies of opening wilderness areas to mining interests and to development owed more to the sentiments of the first part of that declaration than the second.[16]

Reagan also appointed Gary L. Bauer, another evangelical, to his staff, first as a low-level functionary and later as domestic policy adviser, where he sought to push the Religious Right's "family values" agenda. Beyond that, however, Reagan and his inner circle of advisers devoted far more attention to economic matters, principally tax cuts, and to a deliberate escalation of tensions with the Soviet Union and massive increases in military spending. In a speech before the annual convention of the National Association of Evangelicals, meeting in Orlando, Florida, in 1983, Reagan asked for the continued support of evangelicals, invoking the specter of communism and resorting to the language of dualism. He urged his evangelical supporters to "speak out against

---

16. Quoted in George Vecsey, "Sports of the Times: Wildlife Group Fights U.S. Policy," *New York Times*, August 22, 1981.

those who would place the United States in a position of military and moral inferiority" and to resist "the temptation of blithely declaring yourselves above it all and label both sides equally at fault, to ignore the facts of history and the aggressive impulses of an evil empire, to simply call the arms race a giant misunderstanding and thereby remove yourself from the struggle between right and wrong and good and evil."[17]

The Reagan administration's preoccupation with the economy and with the Soviet Union, however, came at the price of neglecting other elements of the Religious Right agenda. This was part of a conscious strategy to defer action on those matters until other priorities could be addressed. Reagan, for example, refused to push for the proposed Human Life Statute in 1981 or the Family Protection Act of 1981, both of which would have outlawed abortion.[18]

The failure of the Reagan administration to prosecute the agenda of the Religious Right as vigorously as its leaders had every right to expect that he would created a keen sense of disappointment on the part of the Religious Right. "Immediately after Ronald Reagan was elected," Paul Weyrich recalled in 1990, "the administration announced that its social agenda would have to be postponed for several years." Weyrich said that he initiated a conference call with Religious Right leaders at the time and told them, "'This cannot be tolerated. If the idea that economic issues are more important than moral issues takes hold, then it

---

17. John Woolley and Gerhard Peters, *The American Presidency Project* [online]. Santa Barbara, CA: University of California (hosted), Gerhard Peters (database). http://www.presidency.ucsb.edu/ws/?pid=41023.

18. Smith, *Faith and the Presidency*, 349.

says something about what we stand for.'" Weyrich insisted that his warnings went unheeded.[19]

Reflecting back on what he considered the failure of leaders of the Religious Right to advance their agenda during the administration of a president they deemed friendly to their interests, Weyrich blamed the leaders for settling for mere access rather than influence. "What overshadowed all their concerns was simply their pleasure in being able to get in even the back door of the White House," he said. "They didn't want to do anything to jeopardize that."[20]

However Reagan may have disappointed the leaders of the Religious Right, a majority of evangelicals remained loyal. The March 30, 1981, attempt on Reagan's life, just a few weeks into his tenure as president, reinforced his popularity, especially when he handled the incident with such grace and courage. Evangelicals overwhelmingly supported Reagan again in 1984 when he ran against Walter F. Mondale, Carter's vice president. "I don't know if I've been born again, but I know I was born into a Christian family," Mondale declared in the first presidential debate. Noting that his father had been a Methodist minister, Mondale said, "I have a deep religious faith."[21]

That statement—and Mondale's perception that such a statement was necessary or at least might help him politically—suggests that the Jimmy Carter style of religious declaration was still

---

19. Michael Cromartie, ed., *No Longer Exiles: The Religious New Right in American Politics* (Washington, DC: Ethics and Public Policy Center, 1993), 53.

20. Cromartie, *No Longer Exiles,* 54. Cf. William Martin, "How Reagan Wowed Evangelicals," *Christianity Today,* August 2004, 48–49.

21. Quoted in Smith, *Faith and the Presidency,* 346.

very much part of the lexicon of presidential candidates during the 1980s. Mondale, however, perceived the dangers of such declarations. In the same debate, he criticized the "growing tendency to try to use one's own personal interpretation of faith politically," and he especially denounced any attempt "to use the instrumentalities of government to impose those views on others."[22]

Reagan won reelection in a landslide, with 59 percent of the popular vote. Even Mondale's choice of Geraldine Ferraro as his running mate, the first time a woman had ever been a major-party nominee, failed to energize the campaign in the Democrats' favor. Most evangelicals stayed in the Republican camp, and they remained loyal through the turbulence and scandals of Reagan's second term.

In the Iran-Contra affair, the Reagan administration agreed to sell arms covertly to Iran to assist with its war against Iraq; in exchange, the Iranians would release American hostages, and profits from the sale of arms financed the activities of the *contras* of Central America, in defiance of congressional legislation that prohibited the support of insurgent forces in Central America. Reagan, whom Representative Patricia Schroeder of Colorado once referred to as the "Teflon president," was not seriously tarnished by the Iran-Contra scandal, despite the fact that several of his aides were indicted for conspiracy, fraud, and theft of government funds.

The failure of the Reagans regularly to attend church and the revelation that Nancy Reagan consulted an astrologer in the formulation of her husband's schedule might have eroded support among some religious voters. But Reagan shrugged it off, and so did they. By the time he left office on January 20, 1989, Ronald

---

22. Quoted in Smith, *Faith and the Presidency,* 346.

Reagan had achieved almost iconic status among many American evangelicals, despite the fact that he failed to deliver on his central promises to the Religious Right, the outlawing of abortion and the restoration of public prayer in public schools. Even his initial appointment to the Supreme Court, Sandra Day O'Connor, the first woman, disappointed the leaders of the Religious Right because of her qualified support for abortion rights.

George H. W. Bush, a cradle Episcopalian, hoped to inherit the religious voters who had been so loyal to Reagan. Although Jerry Falwell had declared his allegiance to Bush well in advance of the 1988 presidential primaries—and Bush reciprocated by referring to Falwell as a "great friend"—other leaders of the Religious Right remained suspicious of this blue-blood Episcopalian who had been a "pro-choice" Republican until Reagan tapped him to be his running mate in the summer of 1980.[23]

Still another leader of the Religious Right, Pat Robertson, mounted his own bid for the Republican presidential nomination. Robertson finished second in the Iowa precinct caucuses in January 1988, behind Senator Robert Dole of Kansas and ahead of Bush, the eventual nominee. Because of his surprising showing in Iowa, Robertson encountered more scrutiny from the media going into the New Hampshire primary the following week. Although Robertson bristled at being called a "televangelist," mem-

---

23. Letter, George Bush to Ed Briggs (Religion Newswriters Association), June 8, 1989, WHORM: Subject File, Bush Presidential Records, George Bush Library. I am uncertain about the precise location of this file because I requested access to this letter under the Freedom of Information Act while I was doing research at the Bush Library. It was released and sent to me subsequent to my visit.

bers of the press found clips of Robertson speaking in tongues and praying to divert hurricanes on his television program, *The 700 Club*. He fared poorly in New Hampshire and in South Carolina and soon dropped out of the race.[24]

With the nomination assured, Bush turned his attention to his Democratic opponent, Michael S. Dukakis, governor of Massachusetts. Described by Garry Wills as America's first truly secular major-party candidate for president, Dukakis displayed little passion on the stump. The 1988 campaign, generally regarded as one of the nastiest in history, was marked by the Bush camp's notorious Willie Horton ads, which unabashedly played on racial fears. Despite Bush's acceptance-speech pledge of a "kinder, gentler nation," his campaign ran commercials that linked Dukakis to a black murderer who raped a Maryland woman while on weekend furlough from a Massachusetts prison (a program initiated by Dukakis's Republican predecessor as governor). Lee Atwater, one of Bush's campaign advisers, had vowed to make Willie Horton into Dukakis's running mate.

Perhaps the most portentous event at Bush's inaugural festivities in January 1989 was a meeting between Robertson, the defeated candidate for the Republican nomination, and Ralph E. Reed, formerly the head of College Republicans. "My goal," Reed later recalled about his entry into politics, "was to become the next Lee Atwater—a bare-knuckled, brass-tacks practitioner of hard-ball

---

24. For an account of evangelicals' grassroots campaign activity in the 1988 Iowa precinct caucuses and in the New Hampshire primary, see Randall Balmer, *Mine Eyes Have Seen the Glory: A Journey into the Evangelical Subculture in America,* 4th ed. (New York: Oxford University Press, 2006), chap. 8.

politics." Robertson asked Reed for suggestions about forming a grassroots political organization from Robertson's mailing list. Reed drafted a detailed memorandum, and the two men joined forces to found the Christian Coalition later that year. Robertson served as president of the new organization and Reed as executive director.

Four days after Bush's inauguration, Ezra Taft Benson, president of the Church of Jesus Christ of Latter-day Saints, sent the new president a letter recalling his own experiences as Dwight Eisenhower's secretary of agriculture. Benson told Bush that Eisenhower had asked him to open the first cabinet meeting with prayer but neglected to do so for the second, which prompted Benson to send Eisenhower a note. "At a subsequent meeting of the Cabinet, President Eisenhower said, 'If there are no objections, we'll begin our deliberations with prayer,'" Benson recounted. "And that's the way it was with the Eisenhower Cabinet from that time on." In a postscript to his reply to the Mormon leader, Bush wrote, "I asked today that our Cabinet meetings be opened with prayer—sometimes silent, sometimes delivered."[25]

Although Bush had benefited from evangelical votes in 1988, the embrace had been less than enthusiastic. The new president sought to allay their suspicions. "In this world, I have found no greater peace than that which comes from prayer, and no greater fellowship than to join in prayer with others," Bush told the National Prayer Breakfast just a few weeks into his presidency. "As a

25. Letter, Ezra Taft Benson to George Bush, January 24, 1989, OA/ID 19250, WHORM: Subject File, Box 2, Bush Presidential Records, George Bush Library; Letter, George Bush to Ezra Taft Benson (LDS president), January 31, 1989, OA/ID 19250, WHORM: Subject File, Box 2, Bush Presidential Records, George Bush Library.

boy growing up, each morning my Mother or Father would read
a Bible lesson to us at the breakfast table. So I just want to thank
you for letting me join you at your breakfast table this morning."
He concluded, "I would not attempt to fulfill the responsibilities
I now have without prayer and a strong faith in God. And I am
grateful for the many people who have told me that they are praying for me."[26]

Billy Graham, who had prayed at the inauguration, weighed
in with bountiful praise and his advice to ignore "the petty little
comments that some of the wise 'fourth estate' make." "I have
been extremely proud of the way you have handled the Presidency
thus far," Graham wrote in a subsequent letter. "It is amazing and
thrilling. May God bless you and Barbara. What an asset she is!"
E. Brandt Gustavson, president of the National Religious Broad-
casters, assured Bush that, "You are our good friend."[27]

But the relationship between Bush and the Religious Right was
never characterized by genuine ardor. As early as 1990, rumors cir-
culated among evangelicals that "evangelical Christians are being
systematically excluded from and pushed out of staff positions at the
White House." Bush strategists sought to counter that impression by

---

26. Speech, National Prayer Breakfast, Washington, D.C., February 2, 1989,
OA/ID 19390, WHORM, SP507, Box 94, Bush Presidential Papers, George
Bush Library.

27. Letter, Billy Graham to George Bush, February 14, 1989, OA/ID 19390,
WHORM, SP507, Box 94, Bush Presidential Papers, George Bush Library; Let-
ter, Billy Graham to George Bush, May 25, 1989, OA/ID 19590, WHORM,
TR021–04, 048361, Box 17, Bush Presidential Records, George Bush Library;
Letter, E. Brandt Gustavson (president, NRB) to George Bush, November 19,
1991, OA/ID 19252, WHORM: Subject File, Box 4, Bush Presidential Records,
George Bush Library. Graham told *Time* magazine in 2004 that he considered
George H. W. Bush "one of my closest friends" ("10 Questions for Billy Graham,"
*Time,* November 29, 2004, 8).

consulting with Religious Right leaders. Early in 1990, for instance, Lee Atwater hosted a strategy session at the Republican National Committee for evangelicals, the purpose of which, according to an internal memorandum, was "to develop an advisory group to assist Lee in determining party policy through the 90's." The invitation list reads like a who's who of the Religious Right: Pat Robertson; Jerry Falwell; Paul Crouch of Trinity Broadcasting Network; Pat Boone; D. James Kennedy, pastor of Coral Ridge Presbyterian Church in Florida; Beverly LaHaye of Concerned Women for America; Adrian Rogers, president of the Southern Baptist Convention; and Billy Zeoli, Gerald Ford's religious adviser.[28]

In the run-up to the Persian Gulf War in 1991, Bush publicly agonized over the decision to deploy military forces to the Middle East. "The decision I face is perhaps the most critical since WWII," the president told one correspondent in a handwritten letter. During a meeting with Bush at the White House, Edmund Browning, the presiding bishop of the Episcopal Church, counseled restraint in the course of a vigorous exchange. Bush ignored that advice, later remarking to William Bennett about Browning that "I am more convinced than ever that he is fundamentally wrong."[29]

---

28. Letter, Mike W. Perry, National Writers Group, Seattle, to George Bush, October 30, 1990, OA/ID 19249, WHORM: Subject File, Box 1, Bush Presidential Records, George Bush Library; Facsimile, Department of Health & Human Services letterhead to Doug Wead, January 23, 1990, OA/ID 40363, White House Office of Public Liaison, Leigh Ann Metzger files, Bush Presidential Records, George Bush Library.

29. Letter [handwritten], George Bush to Susan Gianonno (*Young and Republican,* New York), December 21, 1990, OA/ID 17570, WHORM: Subject File, FG001–07, Box 43, Bush Presidential Records, George Bush Library; Letter, George Bush to William Bennett, February 23, 1991, OA/ID 17570, WHORM: Subject File, FG001–07, Box 56, Bush Presidential Records, George Bush Library.

Bush preferred the counsel of politically conservative evangelicals, who provided him with cover. On the eve of the invasion, Bush invited Billy and Ruth Graham to spend the night at the White House, a gesture widely viewed as an attempt to cloak his actions in the mantle of righteousness and thereby to mute criticism. "Just a note to tell you how much I appreciated your recent visit to Washington," Bush wrote to Graham a couple of days later. "You remain an invaluable source of peace and consolation for Barbara and me—and indeed for countless Americans in search of guidance during this difficult time."[30]

"You have handled this crisis with God-given wisdom both diplomatically and militarily," evangelist James Robison enthused in a letter to the president. "Only God could have enabled you to perform in such an admirable manner."[31]

With the possible exception of the Persian Gulf War, the defining moment of the Bush administration was the fall of the Soviet Union, illustrated dramatically with the collapse of the Berlin Wall on November 9, 1989. Ever since the end of World War II, the United States had expended untold resources—economic, military, psychic—in the Cold War. Two wars, Korea and Vietnam, had been waged in an effort to contain the Soviet threat. Schoolchildren in the 1950s and 1960s endured periodic civil defense

---

30. Letter, George Bush to Billy Graham, January 24, 1991, OA/ID 17570, WHORM: Subject File, FG001–07, Box 56, Bush Presidential Records, George Bush Library.

31. Letter, James Robison to George Bush, February 26, 1991, OA/ID 19250, WHORM: Subject File, Box 2, Bush Presidential Records, George Bush Library.

drills that sent them diving beneath their desks in anticipation of a nuclear attack.

Although most evangelicals had been politically quiescent from the Scopes trial of the mid-1920s until Carter's first presidential campaign in the mid-1970s, the one issue that sustained their interest throughout those middle decades of the twentieth century was the specter of communism, usually modified in evangelical parlance as "godless communism." A passel of conservative organizations, notably the John Birch Society, founded by Robert Welch in 1958, sought to combine religion with anti-communist and anti-government sentiments. Several evangelicals joined the fray, including Carl McIntire with his American Council of Christian Churches and the Christian Crusade, headed by Billy James Hargis. Billy Graham first caught Richard Nixon's attention because both men were anti-communist crusaders in the late 1940s.[32]

Although evangelicals themselves did not organize politically until the late 1970s, Reagan's warnings about the Soviet menace drew on long-standing fears and enhanced his appeal among many conservative voters. His relentless use of dualistic language—good and evil, right and wrong—resonated especially with evangelicals, whose pastors often employed the same rhetoric. Reagan's speech before evangelicals in Orlando, Florida, in 1983, unequivocally identified the Soviet Union as the "evil

---

32. For an overview of these organizations, see Tyler Thompson, "Those Cries on the Right," *Classmate*, April 1964, 26–28. Hargis was later discredited in a sex scandal; two newly married students from his school, American Christian Crusade College, confessed to one another on their honeymoon that each of them had prior sexual relations with Hargis. See s.v. "Hargis, Billy James," in Randall Balmer, *Encyclopedia of Evangelicalism*, rev. ed. (Waco, TX: Baylor University Press, 2004).

empire," which must be vanquished. In the eyes of the Religious Right, his massive escalation in military spending was as much a religious as a political crusade.

In the face of such a build-up, the Soviet Union could not compete and eventually collapsed beneath its own weight. With the demise of the Berlin Wall, so long a symbol of communist repression, the "evil empire" no longer loomed as such a threat. But the absence of the Soviet menace also deprived Americans of part of the identity they had forged for themselves for more than half a century. It is the nature of human beings and social organizations to define themselves in contradistinction to an enemy. Throughout most of the twentieth century, whatever we Americans were as a people, we knew that we were not "godless communists." The rhetoric of dualism, so attractive to Americans and to evangelicals in particular, assured us that we were a religious people, and, for many, a Christian nation.

The collapse of the Soviet empire in November 1989 robbed Americans of their most durable adversary. Presidential politics in the ensuing decades, and certainly through the administration of George Bush's son, George W. Bush, would be preoccupied with the identification of a new enemy.

Bill Clinton and Jesse Jackson, shown here after Jackson was awarded the
Congressional Medal of Freedom in 2000. Jackson, a Baptist minister, had
mounted vigorous campaigns for the Democratic presidential nomination in
1984 and 1988. Clinton was sometimes referred to as America's "first black
president" because of his evident comfort with religious audiences,
especially African American churches.

By his own account, George W. Bush's evangelical conversion reordered his
dissolute life. His critics, however, questioned how much his religious
commitments informed his policies, especially the invasion of Iraq and the
use of torture against those he designated as "enemy combatants."

# FIVE

# DUALISTIC DISCOURSE

## *The Clinton Interregnum and Bush Redux*

Riding the wave of popularity for his handling of the Persian Gulf War, George Bush approached reelection in 1992 with a 91 percent approval rating in March of that year. His opponent was the Democratic governor of Arkansas, William Jefferson Clinton. Bill Clinton was born William Jefferson Blythe IV, named after his father, who died in an automobile accident before Bill's birth. He grew up in modest circumstances in Hope, Arkansas, and, after his mother's remarriage to a car salesman named Roger Clinton, in Hot Springs, Arkansas. Roger Clinton was alcoholic and abusive; in 1959, in the course of an argument with Bill's mother, Roger Clinton fired a gun in her direction, the bullet lodging in a wall of the house. At age fourteen, Bill finally stood up to his stepfather and warned him never again to abuse his mother. "It was a dramatic thing," Clinton told *Time* magazine in 1992. "It made me know I could do it if I had to. But it made me more conflict-averse. It's a really painful thing to threaten to beat up your stepfather."[1]

Although Clinton's parents attended church only rarely, his mother encouraged him to go. In his autobiography, Clinton describes the Park Place Baptist Church in Hot Springs as "my first real church" and fondly remembers his Sunday school teacher. "In 1955, I had absorbed enough of my church's teachings to know that I was a sinner and to want Jesus to save me," he wrote. "So I came down the aisle at the end of Sunday service, professed my faith in Christ, and asked to be baptized." Clinton joined the church, which was part of the Southern Baptist Convention, at age nine.[2]

Another formative religious experience for the young Clinton was Billy Graham's 1959 evangelistic crusade at War Memorial Stadium in Little Rock. Racial tensions were still running high following the violence that attended the desegregation of Central High School in Little Rock two years earlier; the White Citizens' Council admonished Graham to invite whites only to the meetings. Graham refused. "And it really touched me, because my grandparents, who had no education, particularly, and were very modest people, were among the few white people I knew who supported school integration," Clinton recalled in 2000. "And all of a sudden, to have Billy Graham validating this based on his Christian witness had a profound impact on me."[3]

---

1. Quoted in William A. DeGregorio, 'The Complete Book of U.S. Presidents: From George Washington to George W. Bush, rev. ed. (New York: Barnes & Noble, 2004), 706. Bill Clinton legally took his stepfather's surname at age sixteen.

2. Bill Clinton, My Life (New York: Alfred A. Knopf, 2004), 30.

3. John Woolley and Gerhard Peters, The American Presidency Project [online]. Santa Barbara, CA: University of California (hosted), Gerhard Peters (database). http://www.presidency.ucsb.edu/ws/?pid=1485.

In his autobiography, Clinton remembered that when Graham "gave the invitation for people to come down onto the football field to become Christians or to rededicate their lives to Christ, hundreds of blacks and whites came down the stadium aisles together, stood together, and prayed together." The scene deeply impressed Clinton. "It was a powerful counterpoint to the racist politics sweeping across the South," Clinton recalled. "I loved Billy Graham for doing that. For months after that I regularly sent part of my small allowance to support his ministry."[4]

By the time Clinton entered the arena of presidential politics in 1992 for his match against Bush, he was a well-seasoned politician. He had run unsuccessfully for Congress in 1974, successfully for attorney general of Arkansas two years later, and was elected governor of Arkansas in 1978 at the age of thirty-two. Two years later, however, he was defeated, in part because of a slew of negative ads. Clinton was elected governor a second time in 1982 and then reelected twice, before mounting his campaign for the Democratic presidential nomination in 1992.

Knowing full well the kind of political tactics that Bush had used against Dukakis in 1988, Clinton and his strategists prepared for the worst. They assembled the storied "War Room" in Little Rock to respond to political attacks in a timely—almost immediate—way. One obvious area of vulnerability was Clinton's relationships with women other than his wife. The allegations of Gennifer Flowers, a lounge singer who claimed that she'd had a twelve-year extramarital affair with Clinton, nearly derailed his candidacy. But a joint appearance by Bill and Hillary Clinton on *60 Minutes,* in which he confessed to having caused pain in his marriage, defused the situation.

---

4. Clinton, *My Life,* 39.

The rhetoric of dualism so characteristic of the Cold War, now past, resurfaced in various speeches at the 1992 Republican National Convention. Pat Buchanan, one of Nixon's former speechwriters and a candidate himself for the Republican nomination, celebrated the demise of the Soviet Union as a victory for the Republican Party. "Fellow Americans, you've got to remember, it was under our Party that the Berlin Wall came down and Europe was reunited," he said. "It was under our Party that the Soviet Empire collapsed and the captive nations broke free." Buchanan then segued into a different sort of dualism, explicitly drawing parallels with the Cold War. "There is a religious war going on in this country," he warned. "It is a cultural war as critical to the kind of nation we shall be as the Cold War itself—for this war is for the soul of America. And in that struggle for the soul of America, Clinton and Clinton are on the other side; and George Bush is on our side."[5]

Pat Robertson was equally explicit in the transference of dualistic rhetoric from the Soviet menace to the Democratic Party. "Seventy-five years ago a plague descended upon the world and covered the nations of Eastern Europe like a dark cloud," the telF evangelist began, but "it was Ronald Reagan, George Bush, and the Republican policies which brought Communism to its knees." Robertson then shifted to a new foe, "a more benign but equally insidious plague," one readily identifiable. "Ladies and Gentlemen, the carrier of this plague is the Democrat [sic] Party."[6]

---

5. Republican National Committee, *Official Report of the Proceedings of the Thirty-Fifth Republican National Convention, held in Houston, Texas, August 17, 18, 19, 20, 1992*, 371, 374.

6. Republican National Committee, *Official Report*, 501, 502.

In the course of the fall campaign, Bush accused Clinton of a lack of patriotism for avoiding the draft during the Vietnam War and for visiting Moscow while he was a Rhodes Scholar at Oxford University. In the first presidential debate, Clinton noted that the Republican president's father, Prescott Bush, had denounced Joseph McCarthy when the elder Bush was a United States senator from Connecticut. "Your father was right to stand up to Joe McCarthy," Clinton said. "You were wrong to attack my patriotism."[7]

In a three-way contest that included Texas industrialist H. Ross Perot, Clinton won the general election with a plurality of 43 percent of the popular vote and 370 electoral votes. Because of his ease in talking to church congregations, and especially his rapport with African American voters, Clinton was regarded by some as America's "first black president." Unlike many of his predecessors in office, he regularly attended church in Washington, usually the Foundry Street United Methodist Church. "My faith tells me that all of us are sinners, and each of us has gone in our own way and fallen short of the glory of God," Clinton said in 1992. "Religious faith has permitted me to believe in my continuing possibility of becoming a better person every day. If I didn't believe in God, if I weren't, in my view, a Christian, if I didn't believe ultimately in the perfection of life after death, my life would have been that much more difficult."[8]

The ease with which Clinton spoke the language of evangelicalism doubtless helped him win over some evangelical voters,

---

7. Quoted in Michael R. Beschloss, "George Bush, 1989–1993," in *Character Above All: Ten Presidents from FDR to George Bush,* ed. Robert A. Wilson (New York: Simon & Schuster, 1995). 243.

8. Quoted in DeGregorio, *Complete Book of U.S. Presidents*, 708–9.

especially those who were lukewarm toward Bush. But the leaders of the Religious Right were furious with Clinton for having interrupted their hegemonic access to the Oval Office. They leveled all manner of charges against him. Jerry Falwell, for instance, financed, publicized, and distributed a videotape called "The Clinton Chronicles," which accused the president of various crimes, including cocaine trafficking and arranging for the murder of critics.

Clinton gave his detractors an opening with the Monica Lewinsky affair, which in turn came to light because of a lawsuit filed by another woman, Paula Jones, who accused the president of sexual harassment when he was governor of Arkansas. Clinton's lawyerly casuistry (he had been educated at Georgetown, a Jesuit university) may have been technically true—if you define "sexual relations" solely as penetration. But the popular perception of the Lewinsky matter, a perception that probably didn't even need to be stoked by his critics, was that Clinton's evasion constituted a lie. The fact that his aides and his wife vigorously defended him and then had to retract their defenses as the salacious details of the Lewinsky relationship came to light further undermined Clinton's credibility and created visible strains on his marriage.

Clinton, well versed in the evangelical dualities of sin and redemption, sought spiritual counsel. Throughout his presidency and well before the Lewinsky scandal erupted, Clinton had relied on a small group of Protestant ministers. "It helps me to stay centered," the president told a reporter. "It helps me to keep in a positive frame of mind. It keeps me both humble and optimistic. It helps to have private relationships with people who are trying to help you reach beyond yourself and stay in touch with what really matters."[9]

Clinton's inner circle of spiritual advisers included several evangelicals: Gordon MacDonald, pastor of Grace Chapel in Lexington, Massachusetts; Rex Horne, pastor of the Baptist church in Little Rock that Clinton had attended as governor; Bill Hybels, pastor and founder of Willow Creek Community Church in South Barrington, Illinois; and Tony Campolo, an ordained Baptist minister and professor of sociology at Eastern College (now University) in St. David's, Pennsylvania. "I don't think I've met him where we both didn't pray," Campolo said. "So it's not like the Old Testament king who says, 'Come in and pray for me,' to the high priest." MacDonald said that Clinton had often received harsh advice from his religious brain trust. "I've been in a small group with two or three guys where some pretty candid things were said," MacDonald noted. "He's accepted rebuke. He invites blunt talk."[10]

"In their various ways, I think they think they're ministering to me," Clinton explained. "They're trying to help me deal with

9. Gustav Niebuhr, "Not All Presidential Advisers Talk Politics," *New York Times,* March 18, 1997. In an interview conducted by Bill Hybels at Willow Creek Community Church in 2000, Clinton characterized these meetings: "They all include you asking me point-blank about the state of my spiritual life, and if you think I give you an evasive answer, then you do pointed followup questions. [Laughter] And then—and they all end with a prayer. Most of the time we both pray." John Woolley and Gerhard Peters, *The American Presidency Project* [online]. Santa Barbara, CA: University of California (hosted), Gerhard Peters (database). http://www. presidency.ucsb.edu/ws/?pid=1485.

10. Quoted in John Woolley and Gerhard Peters, *The American Presidency Project* [online]. Santa Barbara, CA: University of California (hosted), Gerhard Peters (database). http://www.presidency.ucsb.edu/ws/?pid=1485.

the life of the Presidency and the life of the country at the same time."[11]

When the details of the Lewinsky affair became public, Clinton turned especially to MacDonald, Campolo, and J. Philip Wogaman, pastor of Washington's Foundry Street United Methodist Church, for counsel. "At least one of us will meet with the President weekly," Campolo told the New York Times. "We will pray with him, study Scripture together and do our best to help him as he searches his heart and soul. We want him to understand what went wrong with him personally that led to the tragic sins that have so marred his life and the office of the Presidency. We want to provide all the help that we can to spiritually strengthen him against yielding to the temptations that have conquered him in the past."[12]

On the morning of September 11, 1998, the same day that the Starr report would make public the salacious details of Clinton's relationship with Lewinsky, the president offered a tearful confession at the annual White House prayer breakfast. "I don't think there is a fancy way to say that I have sinned," he quietly admitted, adding that he well understood "the rock-bottom truth of where I am." The president, who had worked on his remarks until 4:00 that morning, asked the forgiveness of everyone involved. "It is important to me," he said, "that everybody who has been hurt know that the sorrow I feel is genuine: first, and most important, my family; also my friends, my staff, my Cabinet, Monica Lewin-

---

11. Quoted in John Woolley and Gerhard Peters, The American Presidency Project [online]. Santa Barbara, CA: University of California (hosted), Gerhard Peters (database). http://www.presidency.ucsb.edu/ws/?pid=1485.

12. Laurie Goodstein, "Testing of a President: The Counselors; Clinton Selects Clerics to Give Him Guidance," New York Times, September 15, 1998.

sky and her family, and the American people. I have asked all for their forgiveness."[13]

Many of Clinton's critics, including those in the Religious Right, were none too eager to forgive. Even the pastors who offered counsel came in for criticism from evangelical leaders. When a prominent Baptist minister castigated Campolo for spending time with Clinton, and Campolo replied that the president, like everyone else, was a sinner in need of grace, the minister retorted, "Clinton does not deserve grace."

Clinton's enemies, religious and otherwise, pounced on the Lewinsky scandal. Although Kenneth W. Starr, a special prosecutor, had been appointed to investigate possible wrong-doings in the Clintons' real-estate venture, Whitewater, he came up empty. The Lewinsky affair, however, had refocused and reenergized his investigation, and his report to Congress provided the basis for impeachment hearings against the president. The House of Representatives voted two articles of impeachment, the Constitutional criteria for which are "high crimes and misdemeanors." The Senate trial began on January 7, 1999. On February 12, the Senate rejected both articles, one on a 55–45 vote and the other 50–50; the Constitution demands a two-thirds majority for conviction.

Conservatives, including many leaders of the Religious Right, were furious at the Senate's inability to remove Clinton from office. They believed that they had him in the crosshairs, but

---

13. James Bennet, "Testing of a President: The President; Tearful Clinton Tells Group of Clerics, 'I Have Sinned,'" *New York Times*, September 12, 1998.

the Senate failed to pull the trigger. "If there really were a moral majority out there, Bill Clinton would have been driven out of office months ago," Paul Weyrich, architect of the Religious Right, lamented. "I do not believe that a majority of Americans actually shares our values," he added. "We will be lucky if we escape with any remnants of the great Judeo-Christian civilization that we have known down through the ages."[14]

Cal Thomas and Ed Dobson, both of them former acolytes in Jerry Falwell's Moral Majority, chimed in with a book expressing disappointment in the results of the Religious Right's quest for political influence generally and specifically for the failure to remove Clinton from office. The book, entitled *Blinded by Might: Can the Religious Right Save America?*, answered its own subtitle with a resounding No!

For his part, Clinton understood the value of redemption. At the White House prayer breakfast in September 1999, a year after the gathering where Clinton had confessed his sin, he reflected on what he called "one of the most difficult years of my life." Having survived the public humiliation of impeachment, Clinton waxed rhapsodic about grace. "I have been profoundly moved, as few people have, by the pure power of grace, unmerited forgiveness through grace," he said. "Most of all to my wife and daughter, but to the people I work with, to the legions of American people and to the God in whom I believe, and I am very grateful to all of you who have had any role in that."[15]

---

14. Quoted in Robert Stacy McCain, "Titanic Loss of Family Values," *Washington Times*, June 1, 2001; Paul A. Gigot, "New Right Now Sounds Like Old Left," *Wall Street Journal*, February 19, 1999.

15. Quoted in Marc Lacey, "At Prayer Breakfast, Clinton Tells of a Year of Spiritual Recovery," *New York Times*, September 29, 1999.

*   *   *

The Lewinsky scandal and the Clinton impeachment may have failed to dislodge Clinton from office, but they probably played at least some role in deciding his successor. Clinton's vice president, Al Gore of Tennessee, won the Democratic nomination in 2000 and chose Senator Joseph Lieberman of Connecticut as his running mate, the first Jew on a major-party ticket. Gore sought to distance himself from Clinton; his selection of Lieberman underscored that disassociation because Lieberman had publicly criticized Clinton's behavior from the floor of the United States Senate.

Gore effectively denied Clinton the opportunity to campaign on his behalf, despite the fact that Clinton was generally regarded as one of the more tireless and effective campaigners of the past half century. Gore lost both his native state of Tennessee and Clinton's Arkansas. If he had won either of the two, he would have prevailed in the electoral college and been inaugurated president on January 20, 2001. As it was, the disputed voting results in Florida cast the outcome in doubt for weeks until the Supreme Court, in its 5-to-4 *Bush v. Gore* decision, threw the election to George W. Bush.

Throughout the campaign, Bush, the Republican governor of Texas, sought to capitalize on Clinton's behavior. Bush styled himself a "compassionate conservative," a vague appellation that worried some of the Reagan hard-liners, because they feared an expansion of programs for the poor, but drew favorable attention from many evangelicals. More important, however, Bush pledged, like Jimmy Carter before him, to cleanse the temple of the Oval Office, to restore decency and honor to the White House, a pointed reference to Clinton's misbehavior. He offered himself as a model of probity, someone who had forsaken a dissolute life of alcohol abuse in favor of the path of moral rectitude.

Reared in an Episcopal household, which also attended the Presbyterian church in Midland, Texas, George W. Bush was, by all accounts, a party guy at Phillips Academy, at Yale University, and back in Midland, where he was trying to make his fortune in the oil business. Bush ran unsuccessfully for Congress, and his business ventures were failing. Friends in Midland described his apartment as a "toxic waste dump." In the words of his cousin, John Ellis, George W. Bush was "on the road to nowhere at forty."[16]

Bush's 1977 marriage to Laura Welch, a graduate of Southern Methodist University, tamed some of his fraternity-boy behavior and drew him into the Methodist church, but alcohol remained a problem. In 1984, an eccentric evangelist named Arthur Blessitt came to Midland. Since 1969, Blessitt had been carrying a large, wooden cross with him while he preached, believing that Jesus had personally commanded him to "carry the cross on foot" to every nation in the world. During Blessitt's evangelistic tour of Midland, he, Bush, and one of Bush's concerned friends, Jim Sale, had lunch together. Several hours later, Bush prayed and, in the parlance of evangelicals, became "born again."[17]

Bush's conversion, however, apparently did not reform his behavior. His concerned parents summoned Billy Graham to the family's compound in Kennebunkport, Maine, during their son's visit in the summer of 1985. In the course of an evening family

16. Stephen Mansfield, *The Faith of George W. Bush* (New York: Penguin, 2003), 53, 56.

17. Mansfield, *Faith of George W. Bush*, 63–66. Cf. Gary Scott Smith, *Faith and the Presidency: From George Washington to George W. Bush* (New York: Oxford University Press, 2006), 367–68.

conversation with Graham and a private walk on the beach with the evangelist the following day, Bush decided to renew his faith. He started to read the Bible regularly and participated in a study group using a curriculum designed by a theologically conservative organization called Community Bible Study. The following summer, while nursing a hangover, Bush vowed to give up alcohol altogether.[18]

"You know, I had a drinking problem," Bush told some religious leaders after he had ascended to the presidency. "Right now I should be in a bar in Texas, not the Oval Office. There is only one reason that I am in the Oval Office and not in a bar. I found faith. I found God. I am here because of the power of prayer."[19]

This was the persona that Bush was eager to present to voters. As he prepared to run for president in 1999, he summoned a group of prominent pastors to the governor's mansion in Austin to "lay hands" on him. Bush assured them that he felt "called" to run for president. And on December 13, 1999, during a debate sponsored by the *Des Moines Register* in advance of the Iowa precinct caucuses, Bush, in answer to a question, declared that Christ was his favorite philosopher, "because he changed my life." The interlocutor pressed Bush to elaborate. "Well, if they don't know, it's going to be hard to explain," he said. "When you turn your heart and your life over to Christ, when you accept Christ as the Savior, it changes your heart. It changes your life. And that's what happened to me."[20]

---

18. See Mansfield, *Faith of George W. Bush,* 67–73; Smith, *Faith and the Presidency,* 368.

19. Quoted in Mansfield, *Faith of George W. Bush,* 73.

20. Quoted in Smith, *Faith and the Presidency,* 372, 373.

Bush's declaration of faith drew ridicule from abroad; a journalist in London noted that the "scorn on this side of the Atlantic could not have been greater if he'd said Homer Simpson." Maureen Dowd of the *New York Times* characterized her understanding of Bush's thinking: "Why not use the son of God to help the son of Bush appeal to voters?" Noting that Al Gore had also identified himself as a "born again" Christian on *60 Minutes* a few days earlier, Dowd opined: "When you take something deeply personal and parade it for political gain, you are guilty either of cynicism or exhibitionism."[21]

Judging by the immediate results of the Iowa precinct caucuses, where Bush finished ahead of the rest of the field, and by his winning the Republican nomination and his victory (albeit contested) in November 2000, many Americans approved of Bush's faith statements—or at least they didn't find them objectionable. Voters warmed to Bush's evangelical narrative of personal dissolution and dramatic redemption. And it is at least possible that they—certainly the partisan conservatives—projected that scenario onto the nation: If Bush could, with Jesus's help, effect his own reclamation from alcohol, perhaps he could rescue the nation from the tawdriness of the Clinton years. Salvation by proxy.

That is a highly partisan reading, of course, and it fails to account for a multitude of other factors: Gore's stiff campaign style, for example; the cyclical demand for change; and what at least one pundit called "Clinton fatigue." The larger point is that, by 2000,

---

21. Quoted in Smith, *Faith and the Presidency,* 373; Maureen Dowd, "Playing the Jesus Card," *New York Times,* December 15, 1999.

the contours of an individual candidate's faith and system of belief had become firmly ensconced in the arena of public discourse.

The 2000 presidential campaign also suggests that the particularities of a candidate's faith or religion matter little, so long as the fidelity appears to be sincere. Gore's running mate, Joseph Lieberman, an observant Jew, was the first Jew in American history to run for national office on a major-party ticket. Because Jews comprise less than 2 percent of the American population in an overwhelmingly Christian nation, some Democrats worried that Lieberman's faith might be a political liability. Not so. Lieberman answered some queries about his policy of refusing to campaign on the Sabbath, and the issue quickly died.

Americans, apparently, if the Lieberman case provides any indication, want their candidates to profess some kind of faith—and they seem not terribly concerned about the particularities of that faith. "Our form of government makes no sense unless it is founded in a deeply felt religious faith," Dwight Eisenhower reputedly declared in 1952, "and I don't care what it is." Some variation of that sentiment applies to presidential politics at the turn of the twenty-first century as well.[22]

The George W. Bush presidency, like many new administrations, foundered in its first few months. Then, on a crystalline September morning, two commercial airliners, gorged with fuel, slammed into the Twin Towers of the World Trade Center in New York City.

---

22. The reason I qualify Eisenhower's declaration is that scholars have debated whether he ever made that statement, although it has been "quoted" often. See Patrick Henry, "'And I Don't Care What It Is': The Tradition-History of a Civil Religion Proof-Text," *Journal of the American Academy of Religion,* 49 (March 1981), 35–49.

Another plane plummeted into the Pentagon, and still another, apparently on its way to Washington, crashed into a field in rural Pennsylvania.

Two days later, as Americans struggled to absorb the meaning of this tragedy, Pat Robertson invited his "dear friend" Jerry Falwell on to his *700 Club* television program to discuss the 9–11 attacks. "I really believe that the pagans, and the abortionists, and the feminists, and the gays and the lesbians who are actively trying to make that an alternative lifestyle, the ACLU, People for the American Way, all of them who have tried to secularize America," Falwell declared. "I point the finger in their face and say 'you helped this happen.'" Robertson concurred.[23]

Falwell and Robertson had long ago descended to the level of self-parody, but the alacrity with which various religious and political leaders sought to assign blame for the 9–11 attacks may also have reflected the eagerness of many Americans to locate a new enemy. Bush obliged. Like Ronald Reagan's invocation of the "evil empire," Bush identified Iraq, Iran, and North Korea as an "axis of evil." Although intelligence sources quickly identified Osama bin Laden and his al-Qaeda organization as the source of the 9–11 attacks, the Bush administration gradually shifted the focus of attention toward Saddam Hussein and Iraq, which he characterized as "an outlaw regime that threatens the peace with weapons of mass murder."[24]

In time, the arguments that Bush used to justify the invasion—Saddam's close ties to bin Laden, Iraq's nuclear program, a

23. Transcript of Pat Robertson's interview with Jerry Falwell, *The 700 Club,* Christian Broadcasting Network, September 13, 2001.

24. Transcript, "President Bush Addresses the Nation," the White House, March 19, 2003.

huge cache of weapons of mass destruction—would turn out to be false and unfounded. But as he moved the nation toward what he characterized as the war on terror, Bush continued to claim the mantle of righteousness against an evil adversary. "We do not know—we do not claim to know all the ways of providence," Bush declared in his 2003 State of the Union address, "yet we can trust in them, placing our confidence in the loving God behind all of life and all of history." In the face of opposition from the United Nations and nearly unanimous opposition from the international community, Bush ordered the invasion of Iraq on March 19, 2003.[25]

In the run-up to the invasion, Bush had catalogued Iraq's supposed threats to the United States and singled out Saddam's practice of torturing his own citizens. "If this is not evil," he said indignantly, "then evil has no meaning." By 2005, however, reports were trickling back that American forces, at Abu Ghraib prison in Baghdad and at the Guantánamo Bay detention camp in Cuba, were torturing political prisoners by means similar to those that Bush had decried as "evil." Alberto Gonzales, White House counsel (and later attorney general), had provided the legal groundwork for the use of torture by declaring the Geneva Conventions "quaint" and therefore anachronistic to the "war on terror." The Bush administration greatly expanded a policy called "extraordinary rendition," the transfer of prisoners to third countries not averse to torture.[26]

---

25. John Woolley and Gerhard Peters, *The American Presidency Project* [online]. Santa Barbara, CA: University of California (hosted), Gerhard Peters (database). http://www.presidency.ucsb.edu/ws/?pid=29645.

26. John Woolley and Gerhard Peters, *The American Presidency Project* [online]. Santa Barbara, CA: University of California (hosted), Gerhard Peters (database). http://www.presidency.ucsb.edu/ws/?pid=29645.

Americans' disillusionment with the war in Iraq, and especially the deceptions used to justify the invasion, made George W. Bush, the incumbent, unusually vulnerable when he ran again in 2004. The Democrats nominated John Kerry, United States senator from Massachusetts, a decorated veteran from the Vietnam War, and a Roman Catholic. Kerry's mother was Episcopalian and his father Catholic. "I thought of being a priest," he recalled. "I was an altar boy and prayed all the time. I was very centered around the Mass and the church."[27]

Kerry became interested in civil rights and social justice, in part because of the influence of a black Episcopal priest, Richard Walker, during his school days at St. Paul's boarding school. As such, Kerry became interested in issues of poverty, civil rights, immigration, and the environment. Yet, like other New Englanders, he tended to be relatively taciturn about his faith. In a December 2003 interview, Kerry talked about faith in almost abstract terms, calling it "your guidepost, your sort of moral compass, your sustaining force if you will, in everything that you do." But, he added, "maybe it's a little bit the New Englander in me or something—you wear it in your heart and in your soul, not necessarily on your sleeve." Kerry acknowledged "all the lessons of a lifetime of my relationship as a person of faith, but not something that I think you ought to push at people every single day in the secular world."[28]

On the campaign trail, Kerry carried with him a rosary, a prayer book, and a medal of St. Christopher, patron saint for travelers. Regular attendance at mass was so important to him

27. Quoted in Deborah Caldwell, "Not a Prodigal Son," Beliefnet.com. In the course of the campaign, Kerry learned that his paternal great-grandfather was Jewish.

28. Quoted in Caldwell, "Not a Prodigal Son," Beliefnet.com.

that he instructed aides to make room for it within his schedule. Yet Kerry's access to Catholic mass became an issue during the 2004 presidential campaign. Several conservative bishops threatened to deny communion to Kerry or to any Catholic who did not promise to outlaw abortion. Kerry himself, though politically "pro-choice," made clear that he found abortion itself repugnant, although he did not want to make it illegal. "I oppose abortion, personally," he declared during the campaign. "I don't like abortion. I believe life does begin at conception."[29]

Several of the bishops refused to be placated, and Kerry's prospects among Catholics and other conservative voters were probably hurt by a February ruling from the supreme court of Massachusetts, Kerry's home state, enjoining the state legislature to allow for same-sex marriages. Although Kerry supported civil unions, he opposed gay marriage, a fine point lost in the heat of the presidential campaign. The Bush operatives jumped on the issue, and referenda on the definition of marriage as between and man and a woman appeared on the ballots of important swing states.

The Republican National Committee also declared that Kerry was "wrong for Catholics," an apparent effort to pry votes away from the Democratic candidate. One zealous Catholic in California filed heresy charges against Kerry because he remained "pro-choice." Kerry's defenders labored to point out that not only did Catholic social teaching oppose abortion, the Vatican also opposed capital punishment and the invasion of Iraq, positions supported by

---

29. Quoted in Caldwell, "Not a Prodigal Son," Beliefnet.com.

30. Karen Tumulty and Perry Bacon Jr., "A Test of Kerry's Faith," Time, April 5, 2004.

many Roman Catholic members of Congress who happened to be Republicans.[30]

For his part, Kerry questioned the sincerity of Bush's faith. Speaking at a Mississippi church during the course of the campaign, he suggested that Bush did not practice the "compassionate conservatism" he preached. To make his point, Kerry quoted James 2:14, "What good is it, my brothers, if a man claims to have faith but has no deeds?"[31]

Despite his New England reserve about matters he considered personal, Kerry sought to encourage religious sentiments and to quell the rhetoric of dualism. "And let me say it plainly," he said in his acceptance speech at the Democratic National Convention, "we welcome people of faith. America is not us and them." The candidate continued: "I don't wear my religion on my sleeve, but faith has given me values and hope to live by, from Vietnam to this day, from Sunday to Sunday."[32]

In Kerry's autobiography, *A Call to Service,* he invoked the example of a previous Democratic senator from Massachusetts, John F. Kennedy. He "helped make religious affiliation a nonissue in American politics," Kerry wrote. "It should stay that way."[33]

Kerry lost to Bush in a second consecutive close—and, once again, disputed—presidential election. Had Kerry prevailed, he

---

31. Quoted in James Carroll, "Kerry's Catholicism," *Boston Globe,* September 28, 2004; Julia Duin, "Kerry Cited in Catholic Heresy Case," *Washington Times,* n.d. [2004].

32. "Text of John Kerry's Acceptance Speech at the Democratic National Convention," *Washington Post,* July 29, 2004.

33. John Kerry, *A Call to Service* (New York: Viking, 2003), 24.

would have been only the second Roman Catholic elected president of the United States, after Kennedy. Kerry's preference that religious affiliation would be "a nonissue in American politics," however, sounded almost quaint in 2004. And his refusal to speak openly about his own faith probably constituted one of several tactical miscalculations in his campaign, along with his reluctance to respond to attacks on his military service and his failure to disavow his vote in favor of invading Iraq, in light of the now-discredited justifications coming from the Bush administration.

George W. Bush, on the other hand, spoke freely and openly about his religious views, and he made repeated appeals to people of faith. By 2004, forty-four years after Kennedy's speech at the Rice Hotel in Houston, the rhetoric of religion had become part of the argot of campaign discourse. Although Jimmy Carter had introduced the language of personal piety into presidential politics, at least in the modern era, the Republican Party had seized the initiative, beginning with Ronald Reagan and abetted by the Religious Right.

Kerry, like Michael Dukakis and Walter Mondale and even Al Gore before him, suffered from the widespread impression that Democrats were simply tone-deaf on matters of faith. In close and hard-fought elections like 2000 and 2004, that may have provided the margin of victory for the Republicans, especially when so many issues—the "war on terror," opposition to abortion and same-sex unions—were framed in the language of dualism.

George W. Bush escorts Nancy Reagan to her seat at the National Cathedral in Washington for the funeral of her husband, Ronald Reagan, on June 11, 2004. Four former presidents and their wives attended the funeral.

# CHEAP GRACE

*Piety and the Presidency*

George W. Bush's statement on the eve of the Iowa precinct caucuses that Jesus was his favorite philosopher appealed to many evangelical voters as well as to those who believed that the nation was beset by moral decay. By 2004, Americans had come to expect that candidates for the highest office in the land would open their religious beliefs to the scrutiny of voters. The political muscle of the Religious Right, populated overwhelmingly with evangelicals, meant that presidential candidates sought to speak the language of evangelicalism. Jimmy Carter's declaration in 1976 that he was a "born again" Christian had simultaneously energized evangelicals and sent every journalist in New York to his Rolodex to figure out what in the world he meant. By 2004, the language of "born again" had become a commonplace on the presidential campaign trail.

How different from 1960. John F. Kennedy, trying to dislodge the Protestant establishment, which took faith for granted so long as it was some form of *Protestant* faith, counseled Americans to disregard a candidate's religion when they entered the voting booth. Other issues were far more important, he argued, and besides, the Constitution explicitly prohibited a religious test for office and ensured the separation of church and state. Americans, by a very narrow margin, elected Kennedy to the presidency; his arguments apparently were persuasive to enough voters to overcome previous biases against Roman Catholicism.

Kennedy's case against considerations of faith as a criterion for voting prevailed through the ensuing three presidential elections: 1964, 1968, and 1972. To cite one example of this disregard for candidates' religion, the leading contender for the Republican nomination in 1968 was the governor of Michigan, George Romney, a Mormon. His religion simply did not enter into the political calculus; instead, Romney stumbled politically among primary voters when he declared that he had been "brainwashed" about Vietnam.

The Kennedy paradigm of indifference toward a candidate's faith, having held through the 1972 election, dissolved dramatically following the Watergate scandal and Richard Nixon's resignation. Suddenly, in the wake of the Nixon administration's culture of corruption and Nixon's manifold prevarications, a candidate's faith seemed to matter. It was a perfect opening for a Washington outsider, a Southern Baptist Sunday school teacher who offered himself as a kind of redeemer to a deeply divided nation. Indeed, given his relative obscurity as a one-term governor of Georgia, it's difficult to imagine Carter's meteoric rise to the Oval Office under any other circumstances.

Carter's candidacy reintroduced religion into presidential politics. His pledges of honesty and decency and never to lie to the American people resonated with Americans eager to purge the nation of Nixon, the shame of Watergate, the ignominy of Vietnam, and, quite possibly, the excesses of the counterculture. Carter was manifestly a good and decent man, the voters decided, trustworthy perhaps even to a fault.

The architects of the Religious Right, however, eager to politicize evangelicals, blamed Carter—wrongly—for stripping places like Bob Jones University of their tax-exempt status because of their racially discriminatory policies. They perpetrated this deception in spite the fact that the Internal Revenue Service withdrew Bob Jones University's tax exemption (after years of warnings) on January 19, 1976, fully one year and a day before Carter took the oath of office as president of the United States. Capitalizing on the perception that Carter was a weak and ineffective president, these Religious Right leaders used Carter as a foil to assemble a political coalition in advance of the 1980 presidential election, which featured three major candidates, all of whom claimed to be evangelical Christians.

Ronald Reagan, a divorced and remarried man who, as governor of California, had signed into law the most liberal abortion bill in the nation, won the support of the Religious Right in 1980 and again in 1984. Reagan's checkered past and the fact that his declarations of evangelical faith proved to be somewhat less genuine than Carter's didn't deter the leaders of the Religious Right. With some reservations, the Religious Right supported George H. W. Bush over Michael Dukakis in 1998 and again over Bill Clinton in 1992. Clinton's election represented something of an interregnum for the Religious Right, by now the most powerful constituency in the Republican Party, and the leaders of the Religious Right resented it bitterly. They did everything in their power to defame and to discredit him.

Tragically, perhaps predictably, Clinton played into their hands. Relentless investigations finally produced evidence of lurid, adolescent behavior that led in time to impeachment. The failure of the Senate to remove Clinton from office in 1999 prompted all manner of lamentations and hand-wringing from Religious Right leaders, but they rallied to return to the political arena the following year to ensure the restoration of the White House to the Republican Party.

The introduction of religious language and faith claims into presidential politics raises an important question: So what? Does a candidate's faith or even his moral character make any substantive difference in how he governs?

John F. Kennedy, as we now know, was a notorious philanderer, both before and during his tenure in the White House. Yet his administration, although it was cut short by his assassination, was not beset by any major scandal. Lyndon Johnson's faith was probably minimal, or at least not readily apparent. The one religious principle that guided his life, that the strong should look after the weak, animated his pursuit of civil-rights legislation and his Great Society ambitions; the same principle led to his disastrous prosecution of the Vietnam War.

Despite Billy Graham's repeated attestations to the profound faith and the probity of Richard Nixon, the most telling statement about the depth of Nixon's religious inclinations was probably Norman Vincent Peale's inadvertent remark about Nixon's Quaker heritage. "I don't know that he ever let it bother him," Peale said during the course of the 1960 presidential campaign. In terms of corruption and persistent attempts to frustrate justice and to undermine the Constitution of the United States, the

Nixon administration ranks as the worst in history. Gerald Ford, Nixon's unelected successor, was generally regarded as a good and honest man. His pardon of Nixon, which Ford insisted arose out of his religious beliefs about forgiveness and mercy, probably cost him the election in 1976.[1]

Even his critics would concede that Jimmy Carter was a good and honest man, a person of high moral principle. His performance as president, however, is generally regarded as less than stellar, in part because of his micromanagement administrative style. Since leaving office, and thereby liberated from administrative responsibilities, Carter has been able to act on the peacemaking and humanitarian impulses that lie at the core of his faith. He was awarded the Nobel Peace Prize in 2002; as James Laney, the former president of Emory University, famously remarked, "Jimmy Carter is the first person in history for whom the presidency was a stepping-stone."

Though he rarely attended church, Ronald Reagan was regarded by many evangelicals as one of their own. He failed to deliver on his promises to outlaw abortion and to reinstate public prayer in public schools, but religious conservatives lionized him, in part because of his relentless campaign against the "evil empire" of the Soviet Union. The Iran-Contra scandal, which represented a bold attempt secretly to circumvent Congress by selling arms to Iran and using the profits to support insurgent forces in Central America, never approached the magnitude of the Watergate-era scandals, but it was a scandal nevertheless.

Reagan's vice president, George H. W. Bush, is generally considered a decent man whose administration was not tainted

1. "Religious Issue Stirs Controversy," *New York Times,* September 11, 1960.

by any major scandal. Yet Bush's campaign against Michael Dukakis in 1988 was one of the nastiest in American history, so notorious that Lee Atwater, the man responsible for the infamous Willie Horton campaign commercial, apologized from his deathbed. Bush's pardon of six principals in the Iran-Contra scandal had the effect of frustrating justice; the special prosecutor folded his investigation shortly after Bush issued the pardons on December 24, 1992.

Bill Clinton's womanizing, which nearly became his undoing, was an open secret when he was governor of Arkansas and while he was campaigning for the presidency. His legacy, despite the extraordinary economic growth of the 1990s, will be tarnished forever by his tawdry behavior and by the ignominy of being only the second president in history to face impeachment. Yet, throughout an eight-year presidency and despite relentless investigations, the Clinton administration was not rocked by any significant scandal—aside from the disgrace of Clinton's personal dalliances.

In campaigning for the presidency in 2000, in the wake of the Monica Lewinsky affair, George W. Bush presented himself to the voters as a model of moral rectitude. Like Carter in 1976, Bush used the language of redemption and offered himself as a kind of emetic after the Clinton-Gore years. Since his evangelical conversion in 1984 and his decision to quit alcohol in 1986, Bush's personal life has been, for the most part and at least as far as we know, beyond reproach.

But does probity translate into policy? The record of the George W. Bush administration suggests that it may not. The administration of the man who trumpets his morality deceived the nation (and the world) about the justifications for the invasion of Iraq and went to extraordinary lengths to discredit those who exposed the deceptions. The administration of the man who claims to be a Christian and to embody Christian values ignored centuries of Christian thinking and writing on what is or is not a "just war": Is it a defensive war? Is the use of military force the last resort? Is the amount of force roughly proportionate to the provocation? Is there a reasonable chance of success? Have provisions been made, as much as possible, to protect civilians from being "collateral damage"? The invasion of Iraq meets none of these criteria.[2]

Finally, the Bush administration, which claims to uphold human rights, has authorized the use of torture against those it designates as "enemy combatants." This is the same administration that claims to be "pro-life" because of its efforts to defend the fetus. Yet it engages in the most degrading and demeaning actions imaginable against fully formed human beings.

Does probity translate into policy? The record of the past four decades is mixed. Gerald Ford's pardon of Nixon was an expression of his religious convictions. Jimmy Carter's sense of morality led him to renegotiate the Panama Canal treaties and to draw attention to human-rights abuses around the world. Ronald Reagan's moral compass prompted him to reverse his earlier support for

---

2. There have been some attempts to argue that the invasion of Iraq constituted a "just war." See, for example, Jean Bethke Elshtain, *Just War Against Terror: The Burden of American Power in a Violent World* (New York: Basic Books, 2003). These arguments, however, ignore such crucial evidence as the Downing Street memorandum. As my friend Harry Stout, historian of the Civil War, says, the problem with most modern just-war theorists is that they've never met a war they didn't like.

abortion rights and to advocate a Human Life Amendment to the Constitution.

On the other side of the equation, Lyndon Johnson's personal life would never suggest that he was a paragon of virtue, but he worked passionately for civil rights and sought to improve the lot of those less fortunate. Richard Nixon, hardly a moral exemplar, nevertheless sought to protect the environment and signed several bills that restored lands and a measure of self-rule to Native Americans.

These examples suggest that the quest for moral rectitude in presidential candidates may be chimerical. The candidates' declarations of faith over the past several decades provide a fairly poor indicator of how they govern. Even the record of the two redeemer presidents of the past half century, Jimmy Carter and George W. Bush, is mixed. Carter actually sought to govern according to his moral lights and in fidelity to the principles of decency, honor, and fair play that he articulated on the campaign trail; the American voters resoundingly repudiated him when he ran for a second term. Bush sought the presidency on a platform of morality and Christian virtues. Yet his policies in the first decade of the twenty-first century reflected those values only dimly, if at all.

Perhaps it's time to shift our attention away from the candidates and toward the electorate. What is it we expect from our presidents? Do we look for charisma and political skills, experience in foreign and domestic policy, and administrative competence? Or do we demand that candidates for the White House pass some sort of catechetical test? It's not an either-or proposition, of course, but the record of the last four decades of the twentieth century suggests that we've moved toward the latter and away from the former.

But at what cost? The president of the United States is not a high priest. He or she is commander-in-chief, not pastor-in-chief. Surely it's legitimate to consider a candidate's faith (or lack of same) as an insight into his character, but it should be only one of many considerations. To put it in the starkest terms, when I enter an operating room or board an airplane, my primary consideration is whether the surgeon or the pilot is competent; if I learn that she attended church or synagogue the previous weekend I might like her better, perhaps, or be more inclined to strike up a conversation. But my principal concern is her ability to perform the task I've asked her to do.

Perhaps it's inevitable that in the United States, which has no religious establishment, we look to the president as a kind of moral figurehead, the sum total of our projections about the supposed goodness and honor and moral superiority of America and Americans. We expect the president to be the vicarious embodiment of the myths we have constructed about the United States of America.

But no one—not John Kennedy or Jimmy Carter, not Ronald Reagan or George W. Bush—can shoulder that burden. It's too much to ask of any mortal to be the repository of our collective projections, especially when our assessment of America's standing in the world and our aggregate moral character is so inflated. And yet politicians continually invite us to see them as embodiments of our supposed virtue. They assure us that we Americans are good and moral and decent people, and we need only to elect a good and moral and decent president and all will be well. Foolishly, naïvely, we play along.

And we play along with this cycle of sin and redemption because it offers a kind of cheap grace. We turned to Jimmy Carter in 1976 to purge the nation of Nixon's sins but also to absolve ourselves of complicity. Simply by casting a vote, we could put the whole sordid matter behind us and not trouble ourselves with nettlesome questions about why we, the electorate, elevated Nixon to the White House in the first place. Here was a man whose entire career was littered with dirty tricks and shady dealings, most of which were well known to American voters. Here was a man who seriously compromised civil liberties and who massively escalated the ruinous war in Vietnam. Yet not only did we elect him president in 1968, we returned him overwhelmingly to office four years later. These circumstances raise serious questions about the American voters who put Nixon in office and allowed him to remain there. Simply pulling the lever for Carter in 1976, however, allowed us to evade those questions. Cheap grace.

Bill Clinton's history of philandering was hardly a secret when he ran for president in 1992, but the salacious revelations of his sexual behavior in the White House made most Americans squirm. Rather than ask ourselves difficult questions about our collective tolerance for sexual license and promiscuity in American society, transitory relationships, the endless barrage of sexually themed messages on television, or the easy availability of pornography, we simply pulled the lever for George W. Bush, who offered vague promises about restoring integrity to the White House. Cheap grace.

If the presidency suffers from an inflection of religious criteria, faith itself is also damaged by politicization. Can anyone argue that the integrity of the Quaker faith was advanced by its association with Richard Nixon? Or the Disciples of Christ with Lyndon

Johnson or, for that matter, Ronald Reagan? The two Southern Baptist presidents of the late twentieth century, Jimmy Carter and Bill Clinton, left decidedly different legacies. One left office with his reputation for probity intact, but he was generally considered a less-than-effective president; the other presidency was considerably more successful, especially in terms of balancing the budget, foreign-policy initiatives, and economic prosperity, but probity was hardly that president's forte.

Nearly four centuries ago, Roger Williams recognized the dangers to the faith of too close an association with the state. He worried that the "garden of the church" would be sullied by the "wilderness of the world" if not for a "wall of separation" between the two. Neither Williams nor the founders proposed to bracket an individual's faith from political considerations, but they discerned the dangers of conflating the two.

Although politics has often been described as the art of compromise, the compromise of faith is more perilous, especially in pursuit of political influence. The history of the Religious Right since its inception in the late 1970s illustrates this copiously. The movement, begun as an attempt to defend Bob Jones University and similar institutions against the Internal Revenue Service, later attracted followers by adopting an anti-abortion position as part of its agenda. The Religious Right directed its support to Ronald Reagan in 1980, and beginning with the Reagan administration, leaders of the Religious Right have enjoyed virtually unlimited access to the White House, except for the years 1993 until 2001.

And what does the Religious Right have to show for its identification of the faith with the political process? Precious little. The leaders of the Religious Right have failed to outlaw abortion, their signature issue since 1980, and this despite the fact that the Republicans have controlled both the White House and Congress for most of those years. From February 1, 2006, with the swearing in of Samuel Alito to the Supreme Court, until January 3, 2007, when the new Democratic majorities took control of Congress, for example, the Republican-Religious Right coalition controlled all three branches of the federal government. The chief executive, the majority leader of the Senate, and the speaker of the House of Representatives all claimed to be evangelical Christians and unalterably opposed to abortion. Yet, curiously, they made no attempt to outlaw abortion.

They did, however, manage to pass a bill authorizing the use of torture against those the administration designated as "enemy combatants." And here the danger of prostituting the faith in pursuit of political power comes into bold relief. The same leaders of the Religious Right who claim to be "pro-life," who have anointed themselves the moral arbiters of society, have refused unequivocally to condemn the use of torture. In the course of writing my previous book, *Thy Kingdom Come,* I asked eight Religious Right organizations to send me a copy of their position on the use of torture. Only two replied, and this despite the fact that these groups have detailed position papers on everything from stem cells to same-sex unions. Both of my respondents defended the Bush administration's policies on torture.[3]

---

3. See Randall Balmer, *Thy Kingdom Come: How the Religious Right Distorts the Faith and Threatens America* (New York: Basic Books, 2006), 172–75. At this writing (August 2007), to the best of my knowledge, no Religious Right organization has yet unequivocally denounced the use of torture, although the National Association of Evangelicals finally adopted "An Evangelical Declaration against Torture" (of which I am a signatory) on March 11, 2007, nearly two years after the Bush administration's torture practices came to light.

My reading of American religious history is that religion always functions best from the margins of society and not in the councils of power. Once you identify the faith with a particular candidate or party or with the quest for political influence, ultimately it is the faith that suffers. Compromise may work in politics. It's less appropriate to the realm of faith and belief.

Should a candidate's faith matter to voters? The record of the final four decades of the twentieth century and the initial years of the twenty-first century suggests that professions of religious belief on the campaign trail do not provide a good indicator of how a president comports himself in office. There is, in short, no direct correlation between probity and policy. Jimmy Carter may provide something of an exception to that generalization, but few Americans view his administration with nostalgia, even though he has redeemed himself in the eyes of many Americans with his activities since leaving office. Ronald Reagan evokes a lot of nostalgia, especially among conservatives, but he was singularly unsuccessful in following through on the campaign promises that he insisted were motivated by his religious convictions.

The radical disjunction between George W. Bush's claims of moral rectitude and his indifference to the moral ramifications of his policies is striking, even breathtaking. In the course of his administration, the United States—this "blessed country," in Bush's words—embarked on its first aggressive (as opposed to defensive) military campaign in history, all the while flouting the just-war criteria of the Christian tradition that Bush claims to embrace. The Bush administration also approved the use of torture against "enemy combatants," thereby surrendering much of the moral authority the United States once enjoyed in the eyes of the world.

Should a candidate's faith make any difference to the voters? In this age of full disclosure, exhaustive background checks, and confessional politics, voters know far more about candidates than they did in 1960. More, perhaps, than any sane person should care to know. But are we asking the right questions? The contours of a candidate's faith are fair game as insight into her or his character, but we should also ask probing questions about other matters—economics, foreign policy, social issues—and then *pay careful attention to the answers.* Is there any evidence to believe that a candidate's profession of faith is anything more than window-dressing or a play for religious voters? Is there reason to believe that a candidate's moral compass, even with no religious affiliation or a tepid declaration of faith, will guide his or her decision-making?

The lesson of the final decades of the twentieth century is that voters should approach candidates' professions of faith with more than a little suspicion. Too often, the vetting of a candidate's religion has diverted our attention from other important questions.

Perhaps, once again, our disappointment, our anger, even our outrage is misplaced. Most politicians excel in their chosen line of work because they have learned to discern the mood and attitudes and prejudices of the voters. The most skilled among them find ways to reflect those sentiments back to the electorate. They deal in gauzy, comfortable bromides more often than cold, hard truth. "We campaign in poetry," Mario Cuomo, former governor of New York, once observed, "but we govern in prose."

Among a people who claim overwhelmingly to be Christian, and in a nation where well over 90 percent of us tell pollsters that we believe in God or a Supreme Being, it is no wonder that politicians clamor to speak the language of faith. For many of those politicians, perhaps, the sentiments are sincere; for others, however, considering their actions once in office, the claims seem questionable.

The unwillingness of voters to interrogate those claims and to hold candidates and presidents accountable for their professions of piety, however, renders the rhetoric of religion on the campaign trail meaningless. What would have happened, for example, if there had been a series of thoughtful follow-up questions to George W. Bush's declaration back in Des Moines, Iowa, that Jesus was his favorite philosopher? "Mr. Bush, Jesus demands in the Sermon on the Mount that his followers 'turn the other cheek'? How will that teaching guide your conduct of American foreign policy, especially in the event of, say, an attack on the United States?" Or: "Jesus, your favorite philosopher, says that we should care for 'the least of these.' How does that inform your understanding of welfare or Social Security or civil rights or the graduated income tax?" "Can you provide a specific example of how your fidelity to the Christian faith affected your policies as governor of Texas?"

Then, once in office, a few questions like this: "Mr. President, Jesus expressed concern for the well-being of the tiniest sparrow. Do you see any relationship between that sentiment and your administration's environmental policies?" Or: "Mr. President, Jesus, the man you invoked on the campaign trail as your favorite philosopher, invited his followers to love their enemies. How does that teaching square with the invasion of Iraq or with your administration's policies on torture?"

Other presidents who have made professions of faith should also be pressed to validate their claims. "Mr. Reagan, you repeatedly assured voters on the campaign trail that your religious convictions impelled you to work for making abortion illegal. Yet you have not made any serious attempt to do so. Why not?"

"Mr. Clinton, unlike many of your predecessors, you attend church services most Sundays when you are in Washington and much of the time when you're campaigning. How do you account for the disjunction between your expressions of faith and your private behavior?"

The problem of religiously inflected political rhetoric, it seems, lies not so much with the politicians as with the populace. We allow politicians to hypnotize us with lullabies about faith and morality, and then we fail to take that rhetoric seriously, much less hold them to the principles they articulate so blithely. And when a politician like Jimmy Carter comes along, someone who dares to govern according to the Christian morality he espoused on the campaign trail, we angrily throw him out of office.

What does that say about us, the voters? I think it suggests that we, too, talk a good game about faith and religion and morality, but the rhetoric fails to match the reality. If we were the overwhelmingly "Christian nation" that many claim we are, how could we possibly countenance some of the policies carried out in our name—most recently, for instance, the prosecution of the war in Iraq and the Bush administration's persistent, systematic use of torture?

The answer, it seems, is that our collective affirmations of faith are no more sincere than those of our politicians. We claim to be a "Christian nation," yet we stand by silently as our government conducts an aggressive war in the Middle East that doesn't meet even the barest just-war criteria articulated by Christians through the centuries. Jesus told us to welcome the stranger in our midst, yet that sentiment receives scant expression in our policies on immigration, much less in our attitudes toward those who look or dress or worship differently from us. When we learned about the screams of those being tortured by our government, we raised barely a whimper in protest.

The American form of government purports to be a "representative democracy." That claim elicits all manner of cynicism these days, especially as politicians cavort shamelessly with corporate and moneyed interests in order to finance their elections and their reelections. But on matters of faith, sadly, the United States may well be a representative democracy: The vacuous declarations of faith we hear from our politicians echo our own vacuous declarations of faith. Perhaps our insistence on demanding piety and probity from our politicians is a measure of the deficiency of both we sense in ourselves.

Religion has been bleached out by the bromides of political rhetoric as well as by the comfortable myth that the United States is a "Christian nation." We have been blinded by the false gospel of America's moral superiority, which finds little resonance of late in our policies. Many politicians have proven themselves quite adept at feeding us this pabulum. We devour it shamelessly.

The hypocrisy is overwhelming, but the greater measure of blame lies with the voters than with the politicians, who, after all, merely parrot back to us what they think we want to hear. The solution? One possibility is that we drop altogether the charade of vetting each candidate's faith—which would bring us full circle back to the Kennedy paradigm. "The real issues in this campaign have been obscured," John F. Kennedy complained toward the end of the 1960 presidential campaign. "So it is apparently necessary for me to state once again—not what kind of church I believe in, for that should be important only to me—but what kind of America I believe in."[4]

That is one, perfectly legitimate, approach to the issue of religion and the presidency. It's also an approach not likely to win much support these days.

The other option is that we should hold candidates accountable for their religious rhetoric, mindful that the only honest and effective way to do that will be to hold *ourselves* accountable for our religious affirmations. If voters began to take the rhetoric of piety seriously, politicians would be forced to do so as well.

If we persist in vetting the faith of our presidential candidates, we must find a way to reinvest both religion and the political process with a profundity befitting the importance of both. That, in turn, entails treating the faith claims of candidates seriously and calling politicians to account when they fail to live up to the principles they purport to affirm. If such accountability became part of the political process, chances are that politicians might think twice before offering grandiose protestations of faith, especially when they know that such claims cannot withstand scrutiny.

The larger burden falls on us, the electorate. If we insist on regarding ourselves as a religious people, if we persist in making claims for our nation's moral superiority, then we must hold

4. Quoted in Theodore H. White, *The Making of the President, 1960* (New York: Atheneum, 1962), 391.

ourselves and our nation accountable to the values we espouse. Otherwise, we should drop all pretense of piety, political or otherwise. If we want to view ourselves as a religious people, however, it's not sufficient merely to allow politicians to function as the vicarious projections of our faith. We have to engage in the arduous work of living up to our professed ideals, both individually and collectively.

Anything less is cheap grace.

# JOHN F. KENNEDY
# IN HOUSTON, TEXAS

*On September 12, 1960, in the heat of the presidential campaign, John F. Kennedy, the Democratic nominee and a Roman Catholic, addressed the Greater Houston Ministerial Association on the so-called religious issue that had bedeviled Kennedy throughout the campaign. Kennedy, seeking to displace the Protestant establishment by becoming the first Catholic elected to the presidency, affirmed the separation of church and state as enshrined in the First Amendment to the United States Constitution. He also reminded the ministers that the harassment of Baptist preachers in Virginia had led to Thomas Jefferson's statute of religious freedom. Kennedy's audience that night at the Rice Hotel was respectful but wary; not once was the speech interrupted by applause. The Kennedy paradigm, which urged voters to bracket out a candidate's faith from their considerations as they entered the voting booth, prevailed through the 1964, 1968, and 1972 presidential elections. The Nixon scandals opened the door for the reintroduction of a candidate's faith as a political consideration.*

Reverend Meza, Reverend Reck, I'm grateful for your generous invitation to state my views.

While the so-called religious issue is necessarily and properly the chief topic here tonight, I want to emphasize from the outset that I believe that we have far more critical issues in the 1960 campaign; the spread of communist influence, until it now festers only ninety miles from the coast of Florida—the humiliating treatment of our president and vice president by those who no longer respect our power—the hungry children I saw in West Virginia, the old people who cannot pay their doctors' bills, the families forced to give up their farms—an America with too many slums, with too few schools, and too late to the moon and outer space. These are the real issues which should decide this campaign. And they are not religious issues—for war and hunger and ignorance and despair know no religious barrier.

But because I am a Catholic, and no Catholic has ever been elected president, the real issues in this campaign have been obscured—perhaps deliberately, in some quarters less responsible than this. So it is apparently necessary for me to state once again—not what kind of church I believe in, for that should be important only to me—but what kind of America I believe in.

I believe in an America where the separation of church and state is absolute; where no Catholic prelate would tell the president—should he be Catholic—how to act, and no Protestant minister would tell his parishioners for whom to vote; where no church or church school is granted any public funds or political preference, and where no man is denied public office merely because his religion differs from the president who might appoint him, or the people who might elect him.

I believe in an America that is officially neither Catholic, Protestant, nor Jewish; where no public official either requests or accepts instructions on public policy from the pope, the National Council of Churches, or any other ecclesiastical source; where no religious body seeks to impose its will directly or indirectly upon the general populace or the public acts of its officials, and where religious liberty is so indivisible that an act against one church is treated as an act against all.

For while this year it may be a Catholic against whom the finger of suspicion is pointed, in other years it has been—and may someday be again—a Jew, or a Quaker, or a Unitarian, or a Baptist. It was Virginia's harassment of Baptist preachers, for example, that led to Jefferson's statute of religious freedom. Today, I may be the victim, but tomorrow it may be you—until the whole fabric of our harmonious society is ripped apart at a time of great national peril.

Finally, I believe in an America where religious intolerance will someday end, where all men and all churches are treated as equals, where every man has the same right to attend or not to attend the church of his choice, where there is no Catholic vote, no anti-Catholic vote, no bloc voting of any kind, and where Catholics, Protestants, and Jews, at both the lay and the pastoral levels, will refrain from those attitudes of disdain and division which have so often marred their works in the past, and promote instead the American ideal of brotherhood.

That is the kind of America in which I believe. And it represents the kind of presidency in which I believe, a great office that must be neither humbled by making it the instrument of any religious group, nor tarnished by arbitrarily withholding it—its occupancy from the members of any one religious group. I believe in a president whose views on religion are his own private affair, neither imposed upon him by the nation, nor imposed by the nation upon him as a condition to holding that office.

I would not look with favor upon a president working to subvert the First Amendment's guarantees of religious liberty; nor would our system of checks and balances permit him to do so. And neither do I look with favor upon those who would work to subvert Article VI of the Constitution by requiring a religious test, even by indirection. For if they disagree with that safeguard, they should be openly working to repeal it.

I want a chief executive whose public acts are responsible to all and obligated to none, who can attend any ceremony, service, or dinner his office may appropriately require of him to fulfill; and whose fulfillment of his presidential office is not limited or conditioned by any religious oath, ritual, or obligation.

This is the kind of America I believe in—and this is the kind of America I fought for in the South Pacific, and the kind my brother died for in Europe. No one suggested then that we might have a divided loyalty, that we did not believe in liberty, or that we belonged to a disloyal group that threatened—I quote—"the freedoms for which our forefathers died."

And in fact this is the kind of America for which our forefathers did die when they fled here to escape religious test oaths that denied office to members of less-favored churches—when they fought for the Constitution, the Bill of Rights, the Virginia Statute of Religious Freedom—and when they fought at the shrine I visited today, the Alamo. For side by side with Bowie and Crockett died Fuentes, and McCafferty, and Bailey, and Badillo, and Carey—but no one knows whether they were Catholics or not. For there was no religious test there.

I ask you tonight to follow in that tradition—to judge me on the basis of fourteen years in the Congress, on my declared stands against an ambassador to the Vatican, against unconstitutional aid to parochial schools, and against any boycott of the public schools—which I attended myself. And instead of doing this, do not judge me on the basis of these pamphlets and publications we all have seen that carefully select quotations out of context from the statements of Catholic church leaders, usually in other countries, frequently in other centuries, and rarely relevant to any situation here. And always omitting, of course, the statement of the American bishops in 1948 which strongly endorsed church-state separation, and which more nearly reflects the views of almost every American Catholic.

I do not consider these other quotations binding upon my public acts. Why should you?

But let me say, with respect to other countries, that I am wholly opposed to the State being used by any religious group, Catholic or Protestant, to compel, prohibit, or prosecute the free exercise of any other religion. And that goes for any persecution, at any time, by anyone, in any country. And I hope that you and I condemn with equal fervor those nations which deny their presidency to Protestants, and those which deny it to Catholics. And rather than cite the misdeeds of those who differ, I would also cite the record of the Catholic Church in such nations as France and Ireland, and the independence of such statesmen as De Gaulle and Adenauer.

But let me stress again that these are my views. For contrary to common newspaper usage, I am not the Catholic candidate for president. I am the Democratic Party's candidate for president who happens also to be a Catholic.

I do not speak for my church on public matters; and the church does not speak for me. Whatever issue may come before me as president, if I should be elected, on birth control, divorce, censorship, gambling, or any other subject, I will make my decision in accordance with these views—in accordance with what my conscience tells me to be in the national interest, and without regard to outside religious pressure or dictates. And no power or threat of punishment could cause me to decide otherwise.

But if the time should ever come—and I do not concede any conflict to be remotely possible—when my office would require me to either violate my conscience or violate the national interest, then I would resign the office; and I hope any conscientious public servant would do likewise.

But I do not intend to apologize for these views to my critics of either Catholic or Protestant faith; nor do I intend to disavow either my views or my church in order to win this election.

If I should lose on the real issues, I shall return to my seat in the Senate, satisfied that I'd tried my best and was fairly judged.

But if this election is decided on the basis that forty million Americans lost their chance of being president on the day they were baptized, then it is the whole nation that will be the loser, in the eyes of Catholics and non-Catholics around the world, in the eyes of history, and in the eyes of our own people.

But if, on the other hand, I should win this election, then I shall devote every effort of mind and spirit to fulfilling the oath of the presidency—practically identical, I might add, with the oath I have taken for fourteen years in the Congress. For without reservation, I can "solemnly swear that I will faithfully execute the office of president of the United States, and will to the best of my ability preserve, protect, and defend the Constitution—so help me God."

# LYNDON JOHNSON
# AND THE GREAT SOCIETY

On May 22, 1964, addressing the commencement exercises at the University of Michigan, Lyndon Johnson laid out his vision of a "Great Society," characterized in part by "an end to poverty and racial injustice." Animated by his conviction that the strong had a moral responsibility to care for the weak, Johnson called on his fellow citizens to reject "soulless wealth" and "to shape the civilization." Like John Kennedy, his predecessor, Johnson was especially conscious of the potential of youth. "Within your lifetime powerful forces, already loosed, will take us toward a way of life beyond the realm of our experience, almost beyond the bounds of our imagination. For better or for worse, your generation has been appointed by history to deal with those problems and to lead America toward a new age," Johnson said. "You have the chance never before afforded to any people in any age. You can help build a society where the demands of morality, and the needs of the spirit, can be realized in the life of the nation." Johnson's theological sensibilities were by no means sophisticated. One of the great and cruel ironies of his presidency is that Johnson's belief that the strong had an obligation *to the weak informed both his domestic policies—the "Great Society"—as well as his disastrous prosecution of the war in Vietnam. The latter sapped energy, resources, and credibility from the former.*

President Hatcher, Governor Romney, Senators McNamara and Hart, Congressmen Meader and Staebler, and other members of the fine Michigan delegation, members of the graduating class, my fellow Americans:

It is a great pleasure to be here today. This university has been coeducational since 1870, but I do not believe it was on the basis of your accomplishments that a Detroit high-school girl said, "In choosing a college, you first have to decide whether you want a coeducational school or an educational school."

Well, we can find both here at Michigan, although perhaps at different hours.

I came out here today very anxious to meet the Michigan student whose father told a friend of mine that his son's education had been a real value. It stopped his mother from bragging about him.

I have come today from the turmoil of your capital to the tranquility of your campus to speak about the future of your country.

The purpose of protecting the life of our nation and preserving the liberty of our citizens is to pursue the happiness of our people. Our success in that pursuit is the test of our success as a nation.

For a century we labored to settle and to subdue a continent. For half a century we called upon unbounded invention and untiring industry to create an order of plenty for all of our people.

The challenge of the next half century is whether we have the wisdom to use that wealth to enrich and elevate our national life, and to advance the quality of our American civilization.

Your imagination, your initiative, and your indignation will determine whether we build a society where progress is the servant of our needs, or a society where old values and new visions are buried under unbridled growth. For in your time we have the opportunity to move not only toward the rich society and the powerful society, but upward to the "Great Society."

The "Great Society" rests on abundance and liberty for all. It demands an end to poverty and racial injustice, to which we are totally committed in our time. But that is just the beginning.

The "Great Society" is a place where every child can find knowledge to enrich his mind and to enlarge his talents. It is a place where leisure is a welcome chance to build and reflect, not a feared cause of boredom and restlessness. It is a place where the city of man serves not only the needs of the body and the demands of commerce but the desire for beauty and the hunger for community.

It is a place where man can renew contact with nature. It is a place which honors creation for its own sake and for what it adds to the understanding of the race. It is a place where men are more concerned with the quality of their goals than the quantity of their goods.

But most of all, the "Great Society" is not a safe harbor, a resting place, a final objective, a finished work. It is a challenge constantly renewed, beckoning us toward a destiny where the meaning of our lives matches the marvelous products of our labor.

So I want to talk to you today about three places where we begin to build the "Great Society"—in our cities, in our countryside, and in our classrooms.

Many of you will live to see the day, perhaps fifty years from now, when there will be 400 million Americans—four-fifths of them in urban areas. In the remainder of this century, urban population will double, city land will double, and we will have to build homes, highways, and facilities equal to all those built since this country was first settled. So in the next forty years we must rebuild the entire urban United States.

Aristotle said: "Men come together in cities in order to live, but they remain together in order to live the good life." It is harder and harder to live the good life in American cities today.

The catalog of ills is long: There is the decay of the centers and the despoiling of the suburbs. There is not enough housing for our people or transportation for our traffic. Open land is vanishing, and old landmarks are violated.

Worst of all, expansion is eroding the precious and time-honored values of community with neighbors and communion with nature. The loss of these values breeds loneliness and boredom and indifference.

Our society will never be great until our cities are great. Today the frontier of imagination and innovation is inside those cities and not beyond their borders.

New experiments are already going on. It will be the task of your generation to make the American city a place where future generations will come, not only to live, but to live the good life.

I understand that if I stayed here tonight, I would see that Michigan students are really doing their best to live the good life.

This is the place where the Peace Corps was started. It is inspiring to see how all of you, while you are in this country, are trying so hard to live at the level of the people.

A second place where we begin to build the "Great Society" is in our countryside. We have always prided ourselves on being not only America the strong and America the free, but America the beautiful. Today that beauty is in danger. The water we drink, the food we eat, the very air that we breathe, are threatened with pollution. Our parks are overcrowded, our seashores overburdened. Green fields and dense forests are disappearing.

A few years ago we were greatly concerned about the "Ugly American." Today we must act to prevent an ugly America.

For once the battle is lost, once our natural splendor is destroyed, it can never be recaptured. And once man can no longer walk with beauty or wonder at nature, his spirit will wither and his sustenance be wasted.

A third place to build the "Great Society" is in the classrooms of America. There your children's lives will be shaped. Our society will not be great until every young mind is set free to scan the farthest reaches of thought and imagination. We are still far from that goal.

Today, eight million adult Americans, more than the entire population of Michigan, have not finished five years of school. Nearly twenty million have not finished eight years of school. Nearly 54 million—more than one-quarter of all America—have not even finished high school.

Each year more than 100,000 high-school graduates, with proven ability, do not enter college because they cannot afford it. And if we cannot educate today's youth, what will we do in 1970 when elementary-school enrollment will be five million greater than 1960? And high-school enrollment will rise by five million. College enrollment will increase by more than three million.

In many places, classrooms are overcrowded and curricula are outdated. Most of our qualified teachers are underpaid, and many of our paid teachers are unqualified. So we must give every child a place to sit and a teacher to learn from. Poverty must not be a bar to learning, and learning must offer an escape from poverty.

But more classrooms and more teachers are not enough. We must seek an educational system which grows in excellence as it grows in size. This means better training for our teachers. It means preparing youth to enjoy their hours of leisure as well as their hours of labor. It means exploring new techniques of teaching, to find new ways to stimulate the love of learning and the capacity for creation.

These are three of the central issues of the "Great Society." While our government has many programs directed at those issues, I do not pretend that we have the full answer to those problems.

But I do promise this: We are going to assemble the best thought and the broadest knowledge from all over the world to find those answers for America. I intend to establish working groups to prepare a series of White House conferences and meetings—on the cities, on natural beauty, on the quality of education, and on other emerging challenges. And from these meetings and from this inspiration and from these studies, we will begin to set our course toward the "Great Society."

The solution to these problems does not rest on a massive program in Washington, nor can it rely solely on the strained resources of local authority. They require us to create new concepts of cooperation, a creative federalism, between the national capital and the leaders of local communities.

Woodrow Wilson once wrote: "Every man sent out from his university should be a man of his Nation as well as a man of his time."

Within your lifetime powerful forces, already loosed, will take us toward a way of life beyond the realm of our experience, almost beyond the bounds of our imagination.

For better or for worse, your generation has been appointed by history to deal with those problems and to lead America toward a new age. You have the chance never before afforded to any people in any age. You can help build a society where the demands of morality, and the needs of the spirit, can be realized in the life of the nation.

So, will you join in the battle to give every citizen the full equality which God enjoins and the law requires, whatever his belief, or race, or the color of his skin?

Will you join in the battle to give every citizen an escape from the crushing weight of poverty?

Will you join in the battle to make it possible for all nations to live in enduring peace — as neighbors and not as mortal enemies?

Will you join in the battle to build the "Great Society," to prove that our material progress is only the foundation on which we will build a richer life of mind and spirit?

There are those timid souls who say this battle cannot be won; that we are condemned to a soulless wealth. I do not agree. We have the power to shape the civilization that we want. But we need your will, your labor, your hearts, if we are to build that kind of society.

Those who came to this land sought to build more than just a new country. They sought a new world. So I have come here today to your campus to say that you can make their vision our reality. So let us from this moment begin our work so that in the future men will look back and say: It was then, after a long and weary way, that man turned the exploits of his genius to the full enrichment of his life.

Thank you. Good-bye.

# GERALD FORD'S PREEMPTIVE PARDON OF NIXON

On Sunday, September 8, 1974, a month after taking office following Richard Nixon's resignation, Gerald R. Ford attended St. John's Episcopal Church in Washington and then returned to the White House to address the nation. The president had decided, after consultation with Billy Graham and others, that he would extend a preemptive pardon to his predecessor, an act of mercy that Ford thought necessary for the well-being of both Nixon and the country. Ford, addressing the television camera from the Oval Office, described the plight of Nixon and his family as "an American tragedy," and the new president attributed his decision, in part, to his own religious convictions. Ford declared his belief that he himself would "receive justice without mercy if I fail to show mercy." This brief address illustrates Ford's deep piety and compassion as well as his understanding of the role of conscience in his conduct of the presidency. It also provides a glimpse into Ford's decision-making process. "To procrastinate, to agonize, and to wait for a more favorable

*turn of events that may never come or more compelling external pres-*
*sures that may as well be wrong as right," he said, "is itself a decision*
*of sorts and a weak and potentially dangerous course for a president to*
*follow." The Nixon pardon met with widespread discontent. Jerald F.*
*ter Horst, Ford's newly appointed press secretary, resigned in protest,*
*and Ford took the highly unusual step of going to Capitol Hill, his*
*old haunts as a member of Congress, to refute emphatically and un-*
*equivocally the charge that his pardon of Nixon had been part of an*
*arrangement made prior to Nixon's resignation. Political pundits gen-*
*erally agree that the pardon was a major factor, perhaps the decisive*
*factor, in Ford's failure to win election in his own right in 1976. Ford*
*never second-guessed himself or renounced the pardon; he recognized*
*it as the price he paid for the exercise of conscience. Most Americans,*
*including many who criticized the pardon at the time, eventually ac-*
*knowledged that Ford made the right decision.*

Ladies and gentlemen:

I have come to a decision which I felt I should tell you and all
of my fellow American citizens, as soon as I was certain in my own
mind and in my own conscience that it is the right thing to do.

I have learned already in this office that the difficult decisions always come to this desk. I must admit that many of them
do not look at all the same as the hypothetical questions that
I have answered freely and perhaps too fast on previous occasions.

My customary policy is to try and get all the facts and to
consider the opinions of my countrymen and to take counsel with
my most valued friends. But these seldom agree, and in the end,
the decision is mine. To procrastinate, to agonize, and to wait

for a more favorable turn of events that may never come or more compelling external pressures that may as well be wrong as right, is itself a decision of sorts and a weak and potentially dangerous course for a president to follow.

I have promised to uphold the Constitution, to do what is right as God gives me to see the right, and to do the very best that I can for America.

I have asked your help and your prayers, not only when I became president but many times since. The Constitution is the supreme law of our land, and it governs our actions as citizens. Only the laws of God, which govern our consciences, are superior to it.

As we are a nation under God, so I am sworn to uphold our laws with the help of God. And I have sought such guidance and searched my own conscience with special diligence to determine the right thing for me to do with respect to my predecessor in this place, Richard Nixon, and his loyal wife and family.

Theirs is an American tragedy in which we all have played a part. It could go on and on and on, or someone must write the end to it. I have concluded that only I can do that, and if I can, I must.

There are no historic or legal precedents to which I can turn in this matter, none that precisely fit the circumstances of a private citizen who has resigned the presidency of the United States. But it is common knowledge that serious allegations and accusations hang like a sword over our former president's head, threatening his health as he tries to reshape his life, a great part of which was spent in the service of this country and by the mandate of its people.

After years of bitter controversy and divisive national debate, I have been advised, and I am compelled to conclude that many months and perhaps more years will have to pass before Richard

Nixon could obtain a fair trial by jury in any jurisdiction of the United States under governing decisions of the Supreme Court.

I deeply believe in equal justice for all Americans, whatever their station or former station. The law, whether human or divine, is no respecter of persons; but the law is a respecter of reality.

The facts, as I see them, are that a former president of the United States, instead of enjoying equal treatment with any other citizen accused of violating the law, would be cruelly and excessively penalized either in preserving the presumption of his innocence or in obtaining a speedy determination of his guilt in order to repay a legal debt to society.

During this long period of delay and potential litigation, ugly passions would again be aroused. And our people would again be polarized in their opinions. And the credibility of our free institutions of government would again be challenged at home and abroad.

In the end, the courts might well hold that Richard Nixon had been denied due process, and the verdict of history would even be more inconclusive with respect to those charges arising out of the period of his presidency, of which I am presently aware.

But it is not the ultimate fate of Richard Nixon that most concerns me, though surely it deeply troubles every decent and every compassionate person. My concern is the immediate future of this great country.

In this, I dare not depend upon my personal sympathy as a longtime friend of the former president, nor my professional judgment as a lawyer, and I do not.

As president, my primary concern must always be the greatest good of all the people of the United States, whose servant I am. As a man, my first consideration is to be true to my own convictions and my own conscience.

My conscience tells me clearly and certainly that I cannot prolong the bad dreams that continue to reopen a chapter that is closed. My conscience tells me that only I, as president, have the constitutional power to firmly shut and seal this book. My conscience tells me it is my duty, not merely to proclaim domestic tranquility, but to use every means that I have to insure it. I do believe that the buck stops here, that I cannot rely upon public-opinion polls to tell me what is right. I do believe that right makes might and that if I am wrong, ten angels swearing I was right would make no difference. I do believe, with all my heart and mind and spirit, that I, not as president but as a humble servant of God, will receive justice without mercy if I fail to show mercy.

Finally, I feel that Richard Nixon and his loved ones have suffered enough and will continue to suffer, no matter what I do, no matter what we, as a great and good nation, can do together to make his goal of peace come true.

Now, therefore, I, Gerald R. Ford, president of the United States, pursuant to the pardon power conferred upon me by Article II, Section 2, of the Constitution, have granted and by these presents do grant a full, free, and absolute pardon unto Richard Nixon for all offenses against the United States which he, Richard Nixon, has committed or may have committed or taken part in during the period from July [January] 20, 1969, through August 9, 1974.

In witness whereof, I have hereunto set my hand this eighth day of September, in the year of our Lord nineteen hundred and seventy-four, and of the Independence of the United States of America the one hundred and ninety-ninth.

# JIMMY CARTER'S "CRISIS OF CONFIDENCE" SPEECH

*Widely described—and, at the time, derided—as Jimmy Carter's "malaise" speech, even though he didn't utter the word* malaise, *this address, delivered on July 15, 1979, called on Americans to pull together to solve the nation's ills, especially the energy crisis. (His warnings about Americans' dependence on foreign sources of energy were prescient.) By the middle of 1979, Carter's popularity was low and his presidency listless; just a few weeks before the speech, James Fallows, the president's former speechwriter, had published "The Passionless Presidency," a searing critique of the Carter administration, in the* Atlantic Monthly. *The president clearly took these criticisms to heart. Carter, who had recently returned from a foreign trip, felt that he had neglected his role as America's pastor and had defaulted on his stewardship of the Oval Office, so the speech was meant as a kind of corrective to his presidency. In the course of consulting with his advisers and with "people from almost every segment of our society" about how to rally support for his energy proposals, the president heard a good bit more about what he called a national "crisis of the spirit." Drawing on the long tradition of the American jeremiad, the trope of calling people to repent of their sins and to amend their behavior, Carter's "Crisis of Confidence" speech warned about Americans' "growing doubt about the meaning of our own lives and in the loss of a unity of purpose for our nation." The president cautioned against "fragmentation and self-interest" and commended to his fellow citizens the spirit of sacrifice, which he promised to exemplify by closely monitoring the thermostat in the White House and other measures. "Let us commit ourselves together to a rebirth of the American spirit," the president concluded. "Working together with our common faith we cannot fail."*

Good evening. This is a special night for me. Exactly three years ago, on July 15, 1976, I accepted the nomination of my party to run for president of the United States.

I promised you a president who is not isolated from the people, who feels your pain, and who shares your dreams and who draws his strength and his wisdom from you.

During the past three years, I've spoken to you on many occasions about national concerns, the energy crisis, reorganizing the government, our nation's economy, and issues of war and especially peace. But over those years the subjects of the speeches, the talks, and the press conferences have become increasingly narrow, focused more and more on what the isolated world of Washington thinks is important. Gradually, you've heard more and more about what the government thinks or what the government should be doing and less and less about our nation's hopes, our dreams, and our vision of the future.

Ten days ago I had planned to speak to you again about a very important subject—energy. For the fifth time I would have described the urgency of the problem and laid out a series of legislative recommendations to the Congress. But as I was preparing to speak, I began to ask myself the same question that I now know has been troubling many of you: Why have we not been able to get together as a nation to resolve our serious energy problem?

It's clear that the true problems of our nation are much deeper—deeper than gasoline lines or energy shortages, deeper even than inflation or recession. And I realize more than ever that as president I need your help. So I decided to reach out and listen to the voices of America.

I invited to Camp David people from almost every segment of our society—business and labor, teachers and preachers, governors, mayors, and private citizens. And then I left Camp David to listen to other Americans, men and women like you.

It has been an extraordinary ten days, and I want to share with you what I've heard. First of all, I got a lot of personal advice. Let me quote a few of the typical comments that I wrote down.

This from a southern governor: "Mr. President, you are not leading this nation—you're just managing the government."

"You don't see the people enough anymore."

"Some of your cabinet members don't seem loyal. There is not enough discipline among your disciples."

"Don't talk to us about politics or the mechanics of government, but about an understanding of our common good."

"Mr. President, we're in trouble. Talk to us about blood and sweat and tears."

"If you lead, Mr. President, we will follow."

Many people talked about themselves and about the condition of our nation.

This from a young woman in Pennsylvania: "I feel so far from government. I feel like ordinary people are excluded from political power."

And this from a young Chicano: "Some of us have suffered from recession all our lives."

"Some people have wasted energy, but others haven't had anything to waste."

And this from a religious leader: "No material shortage can touch the important things like God's love for us or our love for one another."

And I like this one particularly from a black woman who happens to be the mayor of a small Mississippi town: "The big shots are not the only ones who are important. Remember, you can't sell anything on Wall Street unless someone digs it up somewhere else first."

This kind of summarized a lot of other statements: "Mr. President, we are confronted with a moral and a spiritual crisis."

Several of our discussions were on energy, and I have a notebook full of comments and advice. I'll read just a few.

"We can't go on consuming 40 percent more energy than we produce. When we import oil, we are also importing inflation plus unemployment."

"We've got to use what we have. The Middle East has only 5 percent of the world's energy, but the United States has 24 percent."

And this is one of the most vivid statements: "Our neck is stretched over the fence and OPEC has a knife."

"There will be other cartels and other shortages. American wisdom and courage right now can set a path to follow in the future."

This was a good one: "Be bold, Mr. President. We may make mistakes, but we are ready to experiment."

And this one from a labor leader got to the heart of it: "The real issue is freedom. We must deal with the energy problem on a war footing."

And the last that I'll read: "When we enter the moral equivalent of war, Mr. President, don't issue us BB guns."

These ten days confirmed my belief in the decency and the strength and the wisdom of the American people, but it also bore out some of my long-standing concerns about our nation's underlying problems.

I know, of course, being president, that government actions and legislation can be very important. That's why I've worked hard to put my campaign promises into law—and I have to admit, with just mixed success. But after listening to the American people, I have been reminded again that all the legislation in the world can't fix what's wrong with America. So, I want to speak to you first tonight about a subject even more serious than energy or inflation. I want to talk to you right now about a fundamental threat to American democracy.

I do not mean our political and civil liberties. They will endure. And I do not refer to the outward strength of America, a nation that is at peace tonight everywhere in the world, with unmatched economic power and military might.

The threat is nearly invisible in ordinary ways. It is a crisis of confidence. It is a crisis that strikes at the very heart and soul and

spirit of our national will. We can see this crisis in the growing
doubt about the meaning of our own lives and in the loss of a unity
of purpose for our nation.

The erosion of our confidence in the future is threatening to
destroy the social and the political fabric of America.

The confidence that we have always had as a people is not
simply some romantic dream or a proverb in a dusty book that we
read just on the Fourth of July.

It is the idea which founded our nation and has guided our
development as a people. Confidence in the future has supported
everything else—public institutions and private enterprise, our
own families, and the very Constitution of the United States.
Confidence has defined our course and has served as a link between generations. We've always believed in something called
progress. We've always had a faith that the days of our children
would be better than our own.

Our people are losing that faith, not only in government itself, but in the ability as citizens to serve as the ultimate rulers and
shapers of our democracy. As a people we know our past and we
are proud of it. Our progress has been part of the living history of
America, even the world. We always believed that we were part
of a great movement of humanity itself called democracy, involved
in the search for freedom, and that belief has always strengthened
us in our purpose. But just as we are losing our confidence in the
future, we are also beginning to close the door on our past.

In a nation that was proud of hard work, strong families,
close-knit communities, and our faith in God, too many of us now
tend to worship self-indulgence and consumption. Human identity is no longer defined by what one does, but by what one owns.
But we've discovered that owning things and consuming things

does not satisfy our longing for meaning. We've learned that piling up material goods cannot fill the emptiness of lives which have no confidence or purpose.

The symptoms of this crisis of the American spirit are all around us. For the first time in the history of our country, a majority of our people believe that the next five years will be worse than the past five years. Two-thirds of our people do not even vote. The productivity of American workers is actually dropping, and the willingness of Americans to save for the future has fallen below that of all other people in the Western world.

As you know, there is a growing disrespect for government and for churches and for schools, the news media, and other institutions. This is not a message of happiness or reassurance, but it is the truth and it is a warning.

These changes did not happen overnight. They've come upon us gradually over the last generation, years that were filled with shocks and tragedy.

We were sure that ours was a nation of the ballot, not the bullet, until the murders of John Kennedy and Robert Kennedy and Martin Luther King Jr. We were taught that our armies were always invincible and our causes were always just, only to suffer the agony of Vietnam. We respected the presidency as a place of honor until the shock of Watergate.

We remember when the phrase "sound as a dollar" was an expression of absolute dependability, until ten years of inflation began to shrink our dollar and our savings. We believed that our nation's resources were limitless until 1973, when we had to face a growing dependence on foreign oil.

These wounds are still very deep. They have never been healed. Looking for a way out of this crisis, our people have turned to the federal government and found it isolated from the mainstream of our nation's life. Washington, DC, has become an island. The gap between our citizens and our government has never been so wide. The people are looking for honest answers, not easy answers; clear leadership, not false claims and evasiveness and politics as usual.

What you see too often in Washington and elsewhere around the country is a system of government that seems incapable of action. You see a Congress twisted and pulled in every direction by hundreds of well-financed and powerful special interests. You see every extreme position defended to the last vote, almost to the last breath by one unyielding group or another. You often see a balanced and a fair approach that demands sacrifice, a little sacrifice from everyone, abandoned like an orphan without support and without friends.

Often you see paralysis and stagnation and drift. You don't like it, and neither do I. What can we do?

First of all, we must face the truth, and then we can change our course. We simply must have faith in each other, faith in our ability to govern ourselves, and faith in the future of this nation. Restoring that faith and that confidence to America is now the most important task we face. It is a true challenge of this generation of Americans.

One of the visitors to Camp David last week put it this way: "We've got to stop crying and start sweating, stop talking and start walking, stop cursing and start praying. The strength we need will not come from the White House, but from every house in America."

We know the strength of America. We are strong. We can regain our unity. We can regain our confidence. We are the heirs of generations who survived threats much more powerful and awesome than those that challenge us now. Our fathers and mothers were strong men and women who shaped a new society during the Great Depression, who fought world wars, and who carved out a new charter of peace for the world.

We ourselves are the same Americans who just ten years ago put a man on the moon. We are the generation that dedicated our society to the pursuit of human rights and equality. And we are the generation that will win the war on the energy problem and in that process rebuild the unity and confidence of America.

We are at a turning point in our history. There are two paths to choose. One is a path I've warned about tonight, the path that leads to fragmentation and self-interest. Down that road lies a mistaken idea of freedom, the right to grasp for ourselves some advantage over others. That path would be one of constant conflict between narrow interests ending in chaos and immobility. It is a certain route to failure.

All the traditions of our past, all the lessons of our heritage, all the promises of our future point to another path, the path of common purpose and the restoration of American values. That path leads to true freedom for our nation and ourselves. We can take the first steps down that path as we begin to solve our energy problem.

Energy will be the immediate test of our ability to unite this nation, and it can also be the standard around which we rally. On the battlefield of energy, we can win for our nation a new confidence, and we can seize control again of our common destiny.

In little more than two decades, we've gone from a position of energy independence to one in which almost half the oil we use comes from foreign countries, at prices that are going through the roof. Our excessive dependence on OPEC has already taken a tremendous toll on our economy and our people. This is the direct cause of the long lines which have made millions of you spend aggravating hours waiting for gasoline. It's a cause of the increased inflation and unemployment that we now face. This intolerable dependence on foreign oil threatens our economic independence and the very security of our nation. The energy crisis is real. It is worldwide. It is a clear and present danger to our nation. These are facts, and we simply must face them.

What I have to say to you now about energy is simple and vitally important.

Point one: I am tonight setting a clear goal for the energy policy of the United States. Beginning this moment, this nation will never use more foreign oil than we did in 1977—never. From now on, every new addition to our demand for energy will be met from our own production and our own conservation. The generation-long growth in our dependence on foreign oil will be stopped dead in its tracks right now and then reversed as we move through the 1980s, for I am tonight setting the further goal of cutting our dependence on foreign oil by one-half by the end of the next decade—a saving of over four and a half million barrels of imported oil per day.

Point two: To ensure that we meet these targets, I will use my presidential authority to set import quotas. I'm announcing tonight that for 1979 and 1980, I will forbid the entry into this country of one drop of foreign oil more than these goals allow. These quotas will ensure a reduction in imports even below the ambitious levels we set at the recent Tokyo summit.

Point three: To give us energy security, I am asking for the most massive peacetime commitment of funds and resources in our nation's history to develop America's own alternative sources of fuel—from coal, from oil shale, from plant products for gasohol, from unconventional gas, from the sun.

I propose the creation of an energy-security corporation to lead this effort to replace two and a half million barrels of imported oil per day by 1990. The corporation will issue up to $5 billion in energy bonds, and I especially want them to be in small denominations so that average Americans can invest directly in America's energy security.

Just as a similar synthetic rubber corporation helped us win World War II, so will we mobilize American determination and ability to win the energy war. Moreover, I will soon submit legislation to Congress calling for the creation of this nation's first solar bank, which will help us achieve the crucial goal of 20 percent of our energy coming from solar power by the year 2000.

These efforts will cost money, a lot of money, and that is why Congress must enact the windfall-profits tax without delay. It will be money well spent. Unlike the billions of dollars that we ship to foreign countries to pay for foreign oil, these funds will be paid by Americans to Americans. These funds will go to fight, not to increase, inflation and unemployment.

Point four: I'm asking Congress to mandate, to require as a matter of law, that our nation's utility companies cut their massive use of oil by 50 percent within the next decade and switch to other fuels, especially coal, our most abundant energy source.

Point five: To make absolutely certain that nothing stands in the way of achieving these goals, I will urge Congress to create an energy-mobilization board which, like the War Production Board in World War II, will have the responsibility and authority to cut through the red tape, the delays, and the endless roadblocks to completing key energy projects.

We will protect our environment. But when this nation critically needs a refinery or a pipeline, we will build it.

Point six: I'm proposing a bold conservation program to involve every state, county, and city and every average American in our energy battle. This effort will permit you to build conservation into your homes and your lives at a cost you can afford.

I ask Congress to give me authority for mandatory conservation and for standby gasoline rationing. To further conserve energy, I'm proposing tonight an extra $10 billion over the next decade to strengthen our public-transportation systems. And I'm asking you for your good and for your nation's security to take no unnecessary trips, to use carpools or public transportation whenever you can, to park your car one extra day per week, to obey the speed limit, and to set your thermostats to save fuel. Every act of energy conservation like this is more than just common sense—I tell you it is an act of patriotism.

Our nation must be fair to the poorest among us, so we will increase aid to needy Americans to cope with rising energy prices. We often think of conservation only in terms of sacrifice. In fact, it is the most painless and immediate way of rebuilding our nation's strength. Every gallon of oil each one of us saves is a new form of production. It gives us more freedom, more confidence, that much more control over our own lives.

So, the solution of our energy crisis can also help us to conquer the crisis of the spirit in our country. It can rekindle our sense of unity, our confidence in the future, and give our nation and all of us individually a new sense of purpose.

You know we can do it. We have the natural resources. We have more oil in our shale alone than several Saudi Arabias. We have more coal than any nation on earth. We have the world's highest level of technology. We have the most skilled workforce, with innovative genius, and I firmly believe that we have the national will to win this war.

I do not promise you that this struggle for freedom will be easy. I do not promise a quick way out of our nation's problems, when the truth is that the only way out is an all-out effort. What I do promise you is that I will lead our fight, and I will enforce fairness in our struggle, and I will ensure honesty. And above all, I will act. We can manage the short-term shortages more effectively and we will, but there are no short-term solutions to our long-range problems. There is simply no way to avoid sacrifice.

Twelve hours from now I will speak again in Kansas City, to expand and to explain further our energy program. Just as the search for solutions to our energy shortages has now led us to a new awareness of our nation's deeper problems, so our willingness to work for those solutions in energy can strengthen us to attack those deeper problems.

I will continue to travel this country, to hear the people of America. You can help me to develop a national agenda for the 1980s. I will listen and I will act. We will act together. These were the promises I made three years ago, and I intend to keep them.

Little by little we can and we must rebuild our confidence. We can spend until we empty our treasuries, and we may summon all the wonders of science. But we can succeed only if we tap our greatest resources—America's people, America's values, and America's confidence.

I have seen the strength of America in the inexhaustible resources of our people. In the days to come, let us renew that strength in the struggle for an energy-secure nation.

In closing, let me say this: I will do my best, but I will not do it alone. Let your voice be heard. Whenever you have a chance, say something good about our country. With God's help and for the sake of our nation, it is time for us to join hands in America. Let us commit ourselves together to a rebirth of the American spirit. Working together with our common faith we cannot fail.

Thank you and good night.

# RONALD REAGAN'S "STATUE OF LIBERTY" SPEECH

The opening of the centennial celebration of the Statue of Liberty on July 3, 1986, provided Ronald Reagan with an occasion to celebrate the themes of patriotism and providence. Speaking from Governor's Island in New York Harbor, Reagan greeted the French president, François Mitterand, and acknowledged the efforts of Lee Iacocca, chair of the Chrysler Corporation, who had headed the fund-raising campaign for the renovation of the statue. "I have always believed there was some divine providence that placed this great land here between the two great oceans," Reagan said, "to be found by a special kind of people from every corner of the world, who had a special love for freedom and a special courage that enabled them to leave their own land, leave their friends and their countrymen, and come to this new and strange land to build a New World of peace and freedom and hope." The president, drawing on the rhetoric of American exceptionalism, invoked the example of the Puritans and cited John Winthrop's famous sermon aboard the Arbella (which Reagan called the Arabella) as the Puritans were

*making the Atlantic crossing in 1630. Reagan paraphrased Winthrop's*
*instructions: "They must keep faith with their God, that the eyes of all*
*the world were upon them, and that they must not forsake the mission*
*that God had sent them on, and they must be a light unto the nations*
*of all the world—a shining city upon a hill." Reagan, who viewed*
*the world in dualistic categories, clearly understood America as God's*
*anointed instrument on earth, the "city upon a hill." This entailed the*
*heavy responsibility not only for providing an example to the rest of the*
*world but also (in another context) for vanquishing the "evil empire" of*
*the Soviet Union.*

Thank you. And Lee Iacocca, thank you on behalf of all of America. President and Madame Mitterrand, my fellow Americans:

The iron workers from New York and New Jersey who
came here to begin restoration work were at first puzzled and a
bit put off to see foreign workers, craftsmen from France, arrive.
Jean Wiart, the leader of the French workers, said his countrymen understood. After all, he asked, how would Frenchmen feel
if Americans showed up to help restore the Eiffel Tower? But as
they came to know each other—these Frenchmen and Americans—affections grew; and so, too, did perspectives.

The Americans were reminded that Miss Liberty, like the
many millions she's welcomed to these shores, is of foreign birth,
the gift of workers, farmers, and shopkeepers and children who
donated hundreds of thousands of francs to send her here. They
were the ordinary people of France. This statue came from their
pockets and from their hearts. The French workers, too, made
discoveries. Monsieur Wiart, for example, normally lives in
a 150-year-old cottage in a small French town, but for the last

year he's been riding the subway through Brooklyn. "A study in contrasts," he said—contrasts, indeed. But he has also told the newspapers that he and his countrymen learned something else at Liberty Island. For the first time, they worked in proximity with Americans of Jewish, black, Italian, Irish, Russian, Polish, and Indian backgrounds. "Fascinating," he said, "to see different ethnic and national types work and live so well together." Well, it's how we like to think of America. And it's good to know that Miss Liberty is still giving life to the dream of a new world where old antagonisms could be cast aside and people of every nation could live together as one.

It's especially fitting that this lesson should be relived and relearned here by Americans and Frenchmen. President Mitterrand, the French and American people have forged a special friendship over the course of two centuries. Yes, in the 1700s, France was the midwife of our liberty. In two world wars, America stood with France as she fought for her life and for civilization. And today, Mr. President, with infinite gentleness, your countrymen tend the final resting places, marked now by rows of white crosses and stars, of more than 60,000 Americans who remain on French soil, a reminder since the days of Lafayette of our mutual struggles and sacrifices for freedom. So, tonight, as we celebrate the friendship of our two nations, we also pray: May it ever be so. God bless America, and *vive la France!*

And yet, my fellow Americans, it is not only the friendship of two peoples but the friendship of all peoples that brings us here tonight. We celebrate something more than the restoration of this statue's physical grandeur. Another worker here, Scott Aronsen, a marble restorer, has put it well: "I grew up in Brooklyn and never went to the Statue of Liberty. But when I first walked in there to work, I thought about my grandfathers coming through here." And which of us does not think of other grandfathers and grandmothers, from so many places around the globe, for whom this statue was the first glimpse of America?

"She was silhouetted very clear," one of them wrote about standing on deck as their ship entered New York Harbor. "We passed her very slowly. Of course we had to look up. She was beautiful." Another talked of how all the passengers rushed to one side of the boat for a fast look at their new home and at her. "Everybody was crying. The whole boat bent toward her. She was beautiful with the early morning light." To millions returning home, especially from foreign wars, she was also special. A young World War I captain of artillery described how, on a troopship returning from France, even the most hard-bitten veteran had trouble blinking back the tears. "I've never seen anything that looked so good," that doughboy, Harry Truman, wrote to his fiancée, Bess, back in Independence, Missouri, "as the Liberty Lady in New York Harbor."

And that is why tonight we celebrate this mother of exiles who lifts her light beside the golden door. Many of us have seen the picture of another worker here, a tool belt around his waist, balanced on a narrow metal rod of scaffolding, leaning over to place a kiss on the forehead of Miss Liberty. Tony Soraci, the grandson of immigrant Italians, said it was something he was proud to do, "something to tell my grandchildren." Robert Kearney feels the same way. At work on the statue after a serious illness, he gave $10,000 worth of commemorative pins to those who visited here. Part of the reason, he says, was an earlier construction job over in Hoboken and his friend named Blackie. They could see the harbor from the building they were working on, and every morning

Blackie would look over the water, give a salute, and say, "That's my gal!"

Well, the truth is, she's everybody's gal. We sometimes forget that even those who came here first to settle the new land were also strangers. I've spoken before of the tiny *Arabella* [*sic*], a ship at anchor just off the Massachusetts coast. A little group of Puritans huddled on the deck. And then John Winthrop, who would later become the first governor of Massachusetts, reminded his fellow Puritans there on that tiny deck that they must keep faith with their God, that the eyes of all the world were upon them, and that they must not forsake the mission that God had sent them on; and they must be a light unto the nations of all the world—a shining city upon a hill.

Call it mysticism if you will, I have always believed there was some divine providence that placed this great land here between the two great oceans, to be found by a special kind of people from every corner of the world, who had a special love for freedom and a special courage that enabled them to leave their own land, leave their friends and their countrymen, and come to this new and strange land to build a New World of peace and freedom and hope. Lincoln spoke about hope as he left the hometown he would never see again to take up the duties of the presidency and bring America through a terrible civil war. At each stop on his long train ride to Washington, the news grew worse: The nation was dividing; his own life was in peril. On he pushed, undaunted. In Philadelphia he spoke in Independence Hall, where eighty-five years earlier the Declaration of Independence had been signed. He noted that much more had been achieved there than just independence from Great Britain. It was, he said, "hope to the world, future for all time."

Well, that is the common thread that binds us to those Quakers [Puritans] on the tiny deck of the *Arabella* [*sic*], to the beleaguered farmers and landowners signing the Declaration in Philadelphia in that hot Philadelphia hall, to Lincoln on a train ready to guide his people through the conflagration, to all the millions crowded in the steerage who passed this lady and wept at the sight of her, and those who've worked here in the scaffolding with their hands and with their love—Jean Wiart, Scott Aronsen, Tony Soraci, Robert Kearney, and so many others.

We're bound together because, like them, we, too, dare to hope—hope that our children will always find here the land of liberty in a land that is free. We dare to hope, too, that we'll understand our work can never be truly done until every man, woman, and child shares in our gift, in our hope, and stands with us in the light of liberty—the light that, tonight, will shortly cast its glow upon her, as it has upon us for two centuries, keeping faith with a dream of long ago and guiding millions still to a future of peace and freedom.

And now we will unveil that gallant lady. Thank you, and God bless you all.

# BILL CLINTON
# ON BILLY GRAHAM

*On May 2, 1996, Bill Clinton hosted a dinner at the White House honoring Billy and Ruth Graham on the occasion of their receiving the Congressional Medal of Honor. In his introductory remarks, the president recalled his youthful impressions of Graham's visit to Little Rock, Arkansas, in 1959, shortly after the violent confrontations at Central High School over the attempts to desegregate the school. Graham, Clinton recounted with admiration, refused to kowtow to the demands of the White Citizens' Council to preach only to white audiences at Little Rock's War Memorial Stadium. Although Graham had made no statement about integration, Clinton was "impressed with the power of his example." For some time thereafter, the young boy sent a portion of his allowance to support the Billy Graham Evangelistic Association. Clinton also remembered Graham's words of comfort to the families of those who had perished in the 1995 Oklahoma City bombing: "He gave what I thought was one of the most honest messages I had ever heard a minister of the Word give." This speech hints at the president's personal regard for clergy. He has often recalled the formative influence of various*

*pastors, and when Clinton faced his own personal and political cri-*
*sis, the Monica Lewinsky scandal, he summoned several ministers for*
*counsel and spiritual guidance, an example of Saint Paul's injunction,*
*quoted by the president, to "bear ye one another's burdens." Clinton*
*viewed Graham and, by extension, faith itself as the embodiment of*
*everything that was good about America. And faith, rightly under-*
*stood and appropriated (as in the case of racial reconciliation), would*
*provide our bearings as we seek both to understand the past and to*
*contemplate the future. Clinton, though he recognized himself as a*
*"poor substitute" for Graham, nevertheless understood himself as act-*
*ing out of similar principles: "A lot of the time what I'm trying to do*
*is get people to lay down the hatreds of the heart and reach down into*
*their spirit and treat people who are different from them with the same*
*dignity that all God's children are entitled to."*

Good evening. The first time I ever met Paul Harvey, he and
his son played through a foursome I was in on his golf course in
Chicago. He never told me the score. But since then he's tried
to tell me the score about a lot of other things. And I've enjoyed
it every time.

To the members of the Graham family, the members of
Congress who are here, ladies and gentlemen: I'm deeply hon-
ored to join with you tonight in honoring two of America's finest
citizens, two of the world's greatest human resources, Billy and
Ruth Graham.

When Billy and Ruth received the Congressional Gold Medal
today, they received only the 114th medal in the 220-year history
of this country. Since, as Paul Harvey said, George Washington
started receiving the first one in 1776, Thomas Edison, Marian

Anderson, Elie Wiesel, Winston Churchill—Billy and Ruth Graham belong in their company, and more.

I am going to make a presentation in a moment related to that, but I wanted to say a few words first. I'm very proud that Billy and Ruth have decided to share this honor with the Billy and Ruth Graham Children's Center of Memorial Mission Hospital in Asheville, North Carolina.

In Galatians 6, Saint Paul said that while each of us must make our own efforts to sustain ourselves, we are also reminded to "bear ye one another's burdens, and so fulfill the law of Christ." Sharing this medal in this way does that. But in so many ways Billy and Ruth have fulfilled the law of Christ, in the ministry of the Word going into all nations.

I hardly ever go to a place, as president, Billy Graham hadn't been there before me preaching. And I feel like a poor substitute from time to time, because a lot of the time what I'm trying to do is get people to lay down the hatreds of the heart and reach down into their spirit and treat people who are different from them with the same dignity that all God's children are entitled to.

Billy and Ruth have practiced the ministry of the deed. Hundreds of times the Bible calls upon us to minister to the poor and the needy as they did in trying to help disaster victims in Guatemala and countless other places. And I know yesterday Billy and I were talking about how proud he was of the work that his son, Franklin, has done, and I saw some of that when I sent our troops into Bosnia and I met some people who had worked with Franklin Graham to try to help the poor children in that war-torn land.

Billy and Ruth Graham have practiced the ministry of good citizenship, being friends with presidents of both parties, counseling them in countless ways, always completely private, always completely genuine. Yesterday we sat in the Oval Office reminiscing and talking about current circumstances, and I asked for Billy Graham's prayers for the wisdom and guidance of God. That is a part of his ministry as well.

Perhaps the most moving example of that came when Billy Graham spoke along with me and a number of others at the first service shortly after the bombing in Oklahoma City. And he knew he was speaking to a vast array of people who had been wounded by that incident. Most of them were Christians, but not all of them were. And yet he sought to speak to all of them, and he gave what I thought was one of the most honest messages I had ever heard a minister of the Word give. And I thought to myself as I watched him give it that only a man completely convicted, completely secure in his own faith, could have looked out at that vast wounded array of human beings and said, "I wish I could tell you that I understand completely why things like this happen. But I don't. Even after all these years, I don't. I don't know why this happened. I don't have an explanation for it. But the God we love is a God of love and mercy amidst all the suffering we are asked to endure. We are not supposed to understand everything but instead to lean on God."

And he made it more powerful because he was able to say to his fellow Americans, "Even after all these years, after I have searched the Scriptures and prayed for wisdom, I do not understand everything. I cannot explain this, but that makes the case for our faith even stronger." I'll remember that for as long as I live.

Finally, I thank Billy Graham and Ruth Graham for the ministry of their life and their personal example, for their extraordinary achievement of five children, nineteen grandchildren, and I think now eight great-grandchildren. If that achievement could be mirrored by every adult in America, we would have about 10 percent of the problems we've got today in this great country of ours.

I thank them for countless personal gestures that demonstrate that as private people they are what they seem to be in public. I thank them for always doing things that will enable them to minister to people they may not even know. I have said this in public before, but I want to say it again. When I was a small boy, about twelve years old, Billy Graham came to Little Rock, Arkansas, to preach a crusade. That town was torn apart by racial conflict. Our high schools were closed there, and there were those who asked Billy Graham to segregate his audience in War Memorial Stadium so as not to roil the waters.

And I'll never forget that he said—and it was in the paper—that if he had to speak the Word of God to a segregated audience, he would violate his ministry, and he would not do it. And at the most intense time in the modern history of my state, everybody caved, and blacks and whites together poured into the football stadium. And when the invitation was given, they poured down together, down the aisles, and they forgot that they were supposed to be mad at each other, angry at each other, that one was supposed to consider the other somehow less than equal.

And he never preached a word about integrating the schools. He preached the Word of God, and he lived it by the power of his example. And one young boy from a modest family for a long time thereafter took just a little money out of his allowance every month and sent it to Billy Graham's Crusade. And I've lived with that all my life.

I'll never forget that when Billy Graham came back to Little Rock thirty years later, probably the most well-known man of God and faith in the world, he took time out one day to let me take him to see my pastor who he'd known thirty years before, because he was dying. And my elderly pastor, with only a few weeks to live, sat and talked to Billy Graham about their life, their work, their trips to the Holy Land, and the life to come. There was no one there. There were no cameras; there were no reporters; there was nothing to be gained. It was a simple, private, personal expression of common Christianity and gratitude for the life of a person who had given his life for their shared faith.

And finally, he got up to go. Billy looked at my pastor, W. O. Vaught, shriveled to less than a hundred pounds, and he said, "Smile, W. O., next time I see you we'll be outside the Eastern Gates." I'll never forget that as long as I live.

So the Congress did a great thing; you have done a great thing; Billy and Ruth Graham have done a great thing in sharing this award with future generations of people who will need their help and their ministry even after they have passed their time on this earth. For all that, as president and in my personal role as a citizen and a Christian, I am profoundly grateful.

I'd like Reverend Graham to come out now, and I will give him a copy of the bill which I signed and the pen with which I signed it. And perhaps he'd like to say a word to you tonight.

# GEORGE W. BUSH
# ON SEPTEMBER 11, 2001

On the evening of September 11, 2001, George W. Bush addressed a stunned nation from the Oval Office. "Today, our nation saw evil, the very worst of human nature," he declared. Resurrecting the Cold War—era rhetoric of dualism, Bush labeled the attacks of that morning "evil, despicable acts of terror" which were leveled against the United States "because we're the brightest beacon for freedom and opportunity in the world." His language recalled Reagan's "city upon a hill" image at the rededication of the Statue of Liberty, and Bush insisted that the United States was singled out for attack precisely because of its virtue. Bush closed his brief, five-minute address with a quotation from Psalm 23, which once again invoked the specter of evil: "Even though I walk through the valley of the shadow of death, I fear no evil, for you are with me." The closing phrase, "God Bless America," long a staple of presidential rhetoric, became ubiquitous after "9–11"—on bumper stickers, in political speeches, even at the ballpark.

Good evening. Today, our fellow citizens, our way of life, our very freedom came under attack in a series of deliberate and deadly terrorist acts. The victims were in airplanes, or in their offices; secretaries, businessmen and women, military and federal workers; moms and dads, friends and neighbors. Thousands of lives were suddenly ended by evil, despicable acts of terror.

The pictures of airplanes flying into buildings, fires burning, huge structures collapsing, have filled us with disbelief, terrible sadness, and a quiet, unyielding anger. These acts of mass murder were intended to frighten our nation into chaos and retreat. But they have failed; our country is strong.

A great people has been moved to defend a great nation. Terrorist attacks can shake the foundations of our biggest buildings, but they cannot touch the foundation of America. These acts shattered steel, but they cannot dent the steel of American resolve.

America was targeted for attack because we're the brightest beacon for freedom and opportunity in the world. And no one will keep that light from shining.

Today, our nation saw evil, the very worst of human nature. And we responded with the best of America—with the daring of our rescue workers, with the caring for strangers and neighbors who came to give blood and help in any way they could.

Immediately following the first attack, I implemented our government's emergency-response plans. Our military is powerful, and it's prepared. Our emergency teams are working in New York City and Washington, DC, to help with local rescue efforts.

Our first priority is to get help to those who have been injured, and to take every precaution to protect our citizens at home and around the world from further attacks.

The functions of our government continue without interruption. Federal agencies in Washington which had to be evacuated today are reopening for essential personnel tonight, and will be open for business tomorrow. Our financial institutions remain strong, and the American economy will be open for business, as well.

The search is under way for those who are behind these evil acts. I've directed the full resources of our intelligence and law-enforcement communities to find those responsible and to bring them to justice. We will make no distinction between the terrorists who committed these acts and those who harbor them.

I appreciate so very much the members of Congress who have joined me in strongly condemning these attacks. And on behalf of the American people, I thank the many world leaders who have called to offer their condolences and assistance.

America and our friends and allies join with all those who want peace and security in the world, and we stand together to win the war against terrorism. Tonight, I ask for your prayers for all those who grieve, for the children whose worlds have been shattered, for all whose sense of safety and security has been threatened. And I pray they will be comforted by a power greater than any of us, spoken through the ages in Psalm 23: "Even though I walk through the valley of the shadow of death, I fear no evil, for you are with me."

This is a day when all Americans from every walk of life unite in our resolve for justice and peace. America has stood down enemies before, and we will do so this time. None of us will ever forget this day. Yet, we go forward to defend freedom and all that is good and just in our world.

Thank you. Good night, and God bless America.

# ACKNOWLEDGMENTS

This project grew out of my long-standing interest in the relationship between religion and politics, two topics that are supposed to be avoided in polite company. I guess I can't help myself. Conversations with a variety of people have helped to guide my thinking over the years, and I'm especially grateful for the comments and suggestions from Edward Blum, Ronald Young, Meredith Weddle, Linda Lader, R. Bruce Mullin, Daniel Vaca, Lowell Livezy, Eric Haugen, and my mentor, John F. Wilson. My father-in-law, Edward V. Randall, provided insights from his vast memory of these years and directed me to useful sources. Once again, my friend and colleague Harry Stout gave this manuscript the benefit of his careful scrutiny. Bill Moyers was kind enough to look over my chapter on Lyndon Johnson, confirm the veracity of the opening anecdote, and offer helpful comments.

I want to acknowledge the invaluable assistance of staff members at the various presidential libraries I visited. I'm especially thankful for research grants from the George Bush Presidential Library Foundation and from the Gerald R. Ford Foundation, a Moody Grant from the Lyndon Baines Johnson Foundation, and a John F. Kennedy Research Grant from the John F. Kennedy

Library. A Mellon Grant from Barnard College helped to defray travel expenses, and a grant from the Leonard Hastings Schoff Fund, administered by the Columbia University Seminars, provided a subvention toward indexing and production costs. Elizabeth Wade provided research assistance, and I'm grateful for the astute suggestions of my editor, Michael Maudlin. He, Lisa Zuniga, and their superb colleagues at HarperOne have expertly shepherded this book to its present form.

My children—Christian, Andrew, and Sara—continue to provide inspiration. Well past the midway point of my threescore and ten, I'm acutely aware of the responsibility I share with all parents to try, even in a small way, to make this world a better place for our children. My generation's record so far has not been sterling; I modestly hope that this book provides a salutary contribution.

Anyone who knows me understands that my greatest debt is to my incomparable wife, Catharine. This book took shape amid the volley of ideas during our morning runs along the Pomperaug River and over a late-afternoon beer by the fireplace. She remains my most challenging interlocutor and my best friend.

—PALM SUNDAY / OPENING DAY
APRIL 1, 2007

# INDEX

# ABOUT THE AUTHOR

Randall Balmer is professor of American religious history at Barnard College, Columbia University, and a visiting professor at Yale Divinity School. He has also taught in the Columbia University Graduate School of Journalism. His commentaries on religion in America have appeared in newspapers across the country, he has been an editor for *Christianity Today* since 1999, and he has lectured at such venues as the Chautauqua Institution, Smithsonian Associates, and the Commonwealth Club of California. He is the author of a dozen books, including *Thy Kingdom Come: How the Religious Right Distorts the Faith and Threatens America* and *Mine Eyes Have Seen the Glory: A Journey into the Evangelical Subculture in America,* now in its fourth edition, which was made into a three-part documentary for PBS. Dr. Balmer, an Episcopal priest, lives in rural Connecticut with his wife, Catharine Randall, a professor of French at Fordham University.